The Badboy Book of
EROTIC POETRY

The Badboy Book of EROTIC POETRY

Edited by David Laurents

BADBOY

Every effort has been made to obtain the proper permissions for the following poems. "All They Want", "To the Seed of the Male of my Species", "Show Hard-on for Blowjob", "If God Had a Mouth", "A Boy's Best Friend", "Tagteam Blowjob", "Touchdown vs. Touch Down", "Jack Off Séance", and "No Doubt" © 1995 by Antler. Reprinted by permission of the Author. "Ecce Homo", "Thanksgiving", and "Jack" © 1995 by Robin Wayne Bailey. Reprinted by permission of the Author. "Upon Julian's Clothes" and "A Passionate Daddy to His Love" © 1995 by David Bergman. Reprinted by permission of the Author. "Encounter" and "Metaphor" © 1995 by Dick Bettis. Reprinted by permission of the Author. "Empire Video" and "from a sky like this" © 1995 by Mark Bibbins. Reprinted by permission of the Author. "Surprising Kisses" and "Hunger" © 1994 by Walta Borawski. From *Lingering in a Silk Shirt* (Fag Rag Books). Reprinted by permission of the Author. "Ejaculation", "On a Subway Pick-up", and "The Danger Zone" © 1993 by William Bory. From *Orpheus in Underwear* (Cythoera Press). Reprinted by permission of the Author.
Continued on page 395.

The Badboy Book of Erotic Poetry

First BADBOY Edition 1995
First Printing December 1995

ISBN 1-56333-382-1

Cover Photograph by Whilhelm Von Gloeden, from the book *Erotic Photographs* (Taschen)

Cover Design by Dayna Navaro

Manufactured in the United States of America
Published by Masquerade Books, Inc.
801 Second Avenue
New York, N.Y. 10017

The Badboy Book of Erotic Poetry

Introduction

"My thoughts are crowded with death" begins Thom
Gunn's poem "In Time of Plague," and that is not what
this collection is about. Elegy is very much a part of the
poetic tradition, and an important part, but this anthology
is a call to remember the pleasures of life, to, as it were,
put the sex back into homosexuality. Death has come to
dominate much queer writing, prose and poetry both; to
many minds, gay and straight, homosexuality has become
equated with AIDS and with death. As I write this
introduction, I am surrounded by death: friends dead or
dying of AIDS, and of other things as well: I have just
learned that one of my writers has thrown himself off a
bridge, and this weekend, I will take a train ride out to my
childhood home and visit the father of my best friend
from high school, who is dying of cancer.

Gunn's poem continues:

and it draws so oddly on the sexual,
that I am confused
confused to be attracted
by, in effect, my own annihilation.

Some of the poems in this book take into account safer
sex; others do not. They are all fantasies, explorations of
the mind, where violence and unsafe practices can be
explored without fear of disease or injury or, for that
matter, commitment.

The poems herein include both the classic and the
new, including many pieces written specifically for this
book and never before published. Permission was denied
us to reprint Auden's pornographic poem, "A Day for a
Lay," certainly among the most famous gay sex poems,
and a great lacuna in this collection. Despite it's having
been first published anonymously and pirated numerous
times, I foolishly asked for permission; Faber & Faber
(whose greed prevented my using either of the Thom
Gunn poems I desired, "The Miracle" or "Courage a
Tale," although I was able to obtain a few poems directly
from Gunn which they did not control) denied me
permission and the estate furthermore threatened to sue if
I proceeded to publish, as had so many others before me,
the poem without permission.

I shall, however, quote two brief samples from this
classic which, in their brevity, constitute fair use in the
context of this introductory essay. This first shows Auden
as size queen, as he describes the fabulous organ of the

boy next door in his characteristic astute and refined
poetic form:

> By soundless bounds it extended and distended, by quick
> Great leaps it rose, it flushed, it rushed to its full size,
> Nearly nine inches long and three inches thick,
> a royal column, ineffably solemn and wise.
>
> I tested its length and strength with a manual squeeze.
> I bunched my fingers and twirled them round the knob.
> I stroked it from top to bottom. I got on my knees.
> I lowered my head. I opened my mouth for the job.

The poem, on the one hand, adheres perfectly to the
requirements of meter and rhyme, but on the other, it
would not be out of place in the pages of a magazine such
as *Torso* or *Honcho*. The poem is as playful in its language,
with much internal rhyme, yet does not sink into
doggerel; Auden maintains a level of raunch appropriate
for any prose pornography. A segment from later in the
poem:

> "Shall I rim you?" I whispered. He shifted his limbs in
>   assent,
> Turned on his side and opened his legs, let me pass
> To the dark parts behind. I kissed as I went
> The great think cord that ran back from his balls to his
>   arse.
>
> Prying the buttocks aside, I nosed my way in
> Down the shaggy slopes. I came to the puckered goal.

13

It was quick to my licking. He pressed his crotch to my
  chin.
His thighs squirmed as my tongue wormed in his hole.

Auden proved that there's no reason poets shouldn't
write excellent and exciting stroke texts, and I've assembled
for your reading pleasure a mix of such poems, by authors
ranging from Pulitzer Prizewinners to Porn Actors, the Old
Guard of poets and the newcomers whose first sales appear
herein. So read through these pages and let these bards of
the bawd get you hard.

David Laurents
New York City
April 1995

Antler
All They Want

Some boys don't care who you are,
    as long as you suck like crazy.
All they want is a blowjob,
    and they want it right now.
The ideals of boylove friendship,
The legacy of boylove in Ancient Greece,
The poetry of cosmic boyhood blowjobs
    means nothing to these lads.
They don't care if you tell them your name.
All they want is your mouth.

They already have boners when they knock on your door.
They don't want to talk. They aren't interested in your
    smile.
Slouched in the chair, spread-legged and stammery,
    displaying obvious boner-bulge,
They aren't interested in your interest in their souls.
Their cocks throb. They can hardly wait.
If you don't stop talking soon,
    they'll unzip their pants,
    thumb forward their dicks
    and sigh, "Blow me, man!"
All that exists in their minds is
    all that a blowjob can be.

Am I supposed to tell them to go away?
Am I supposed to read them the Calamus Poems?
Am I supposed to feel insulted

because to these boys all I am is a blowjob?
Ah, sometimes I think I'd rather be a blowjob
    to a beautiful boy than anything else.
And not just any old blowjob either,
    but the best suckjob of their life.
I'm not fool enough to think
    giving superlative blowjobs to boys
    is any less important
Than introducing them to the Wild
    or talking to them about God.
Indeed, is there anyone left on earth
    that still thinks a priest
    can tell a boy more about God
Than the blowjob-loving mouth,
Than the mouth that loves more than anything
    to suckle his cock
    till it spurts?

Antler
To the Seed of the Male of my Species

How many gallons of semen
    do human testicles produce
    in a healthy life?
Imagine standing under the waterfall
    of all the orgasms of your life
    in an instant!
Imagine swimming naked
    in a swimming pool of come!
How many boys would have to jack off
    to fill a swimming pool to the brim?
Swandive into boycome!
Cannonball into boycome!
Float on your back on boycome
    and spout mouthfuls of boycome to the sun!
Imagine how different America would be
    if rather than cowmilk
    we drank boymilk!
Grade A Boymilk! MMMMMH!
Delivered fresh by your milkboy
    or available in every store!
Each boy is rich with his come!
Each boy has a fortune of come!
Each boy has a free lifetime supply
    of luscious delicious come!
No need for milking machines!
At last a job for American youth
    and cocksucking boylovers everywhere!
At last boys in restaurants as creamers for our coffee

standing naked by tables,
Customers jerk them off
    into their cups.
At last boys in hospitals as nurses
    giving patients a good drink of hot boycome
    before bed.
More fun to see boys and men
    jack off together or alone
    than to see warfilms or quizshows!
More fun seeing boys and men jacking off
    than seeing horse races
    or demolition derbies!
Not till we're more interested in ogling
    semen ejaculating from boy's and men's cocks
    than football or boxing
    is there hope for the future of America!
Not till boycome is served at communion
    will I believe the Father of Jesus
    is the God of Love.

Antler
Show Hard-on for Blowjob

Seeing "Show hard-on for blowjob"
     written above the urinal
          in a highway rest-stop restroom,
I think how many times in my life
     in restrooms at rest-stops,
          libraries, universities,
     parks, bus stations
          I've seen "Show hard-on for blowjob"—
Archetypal universal graffiti
     as much part of every public restroom
          as toilets and toiletpaper,
     state to state, country to country.
Why? Because just as the joy of pissing when high
     under scintillating starrynightsky
          passes from generation to generation
so the mystery and excitement
     of being a young horny guy
          who likes to jack off every day
     and never had a blowjob
to see "Show hard-on for blowjob"
     and think all I have to do
is turn and show my erection
     and the fellow who's taking
so long to piss next to me
     giving me sidelong glances
will favor me with his mouth
     so far down on my boner
my balls look like a

        double bubblegum-bubble
    blown from his lips.
And I'm not even gay, the college student thinks
    on his way home for Thanksgiving
        as his cock gets hungrily sucked
    long after midnight
        at the lonely rest-stop
    in the middle of nowhere.
And I'm not even gay he thinks
    as he cries out ejaculating a
        a gigantic load
    into the tender stranger's mouth
        who after swallowing twice
    gags and come squirts
        all over his face.
Yeah, gay boys and men who write graffiti know
    the power "Show hard-on for blowjob" has
        on heterosexual young men.
Who cares about homosexual dickmeat
    when you can swing on a heterosexual cock
        that not only never got a blowjob
    but was made hard by "Show hard-on for blowjob"
        and turned helpless, shameful, eager
    to show a clean and magnificent erection
        ready to be sucked off?

Antler
If God Had a Mouth

If God had a mouth
I think he'd like nothing more
    than to suck boys off,
But then it occurs to me
    I am God's mouth,
The tongue of God is my tongue
    and every boy's cock is Christ's.
God would rather see Christ get blown
    than crucified,
The cross is not as beautiful
    as Christ's boyhood cock
    spurting in blowjob mouth.
These are the words of Love
    more than the epistles of Paul:
There is more of God
    in blowing a boy with Love
    than all the words of the Bible.

Antler
A Boy's Best Friend

A boy spends more time looking at his boner
Than looking at his face in the mirror,
Enjoys playing with his newsprungcock
More than any other part of his body,
More than reading or listening to music,
More than smoking grass or watching TV,
Just to get off by himself and consult
His miraculous oracle—he is familiar
With its every visage from limp to stiff,
From shrunk from swimming to super-bloated
From many a jackoff holdoff brink, amazing!
What is more fun, more mystical, magical,
Meaningful than those secret chosen moments
Alone with your newgrown pubertydick—
Just you and it!! You know how they say
dog is a man's bestfriend?
A boy's cock is a boy's bestfriend.
A whole night together—a boy delighting
In his beautiful, boundless, insatiable,
Inquisitive, playful, mischievous prick.

Antler
Tagteam Blowjob

How about a tagteam blowjob match
    where Huck Finn and Tom Sawyer
    take turns sucking my boner?
Or how about a tagteam blowjob match
    where I take turns sucking on
    the boners of Huck and Tom?
Or how about my bestfriend and I take turns
    sucking Huck till groaning with near coming
    he tags Tom's outstretched hand
    from blowjob tagteam ring-edge
And it's Huck's turn to look on
    while my friend and I make Tom moan and groan
    wrestling his cock to near coming,
Till finally both boys sprawl voluptuously vanquished
    and my friend and I dance around the ring
    arms raised victorious!
Well, blowjobhunger, boyblowjobhunger,
I think I shall let you continue
    to eat me—
For by blowing boys
I glorify God.

Antler

Touchdown vs. Touch Down

Rather than touchdown in football,
Touch down on a boy's smooth cheek,
  the down called peachfuzz
  that comes before beard.
Who needs football
When there are boyballs?
When a boy can pass his ass
  over your face, his balls
  resting on your eyes?
What better place
For a boy's balls to momentarily rest
  than the closed eyes
  of the boylovepoet?

Antler
Jack Off Séance

Those who want to communicate
    with their lost loved ones
Should gather around a boy's stiff cock
    more than any crystal ball.
Jack Off Séance—a boy's big boner
    illuminated in a dark room,
The guests in a circle around him,
    each gets his chance
    to hold the stiff prick
    and ask it a question.
The answer is in the throbs.
One throb means yes.
Two throbs mean yes.
A boy's full-fledged erection
    is more a medium, more a fortune-teller
    than the most authentic gypsy.
The answer is in the spurts.
To make a boy's cock spurt
    is to make all the dead speak
    in the most beautiful way they could.

No Doubt

No doubt the boy hippopotamus
    longs to frenchkiss
        his boyhood hippo friend.
No doubt boy snappingturtles inspect
    each other's cloacas
        under waterlilypads.
No doubt boy koala bears sniff
    each other's armpits
        when no one's looking.
No doubt boy tube-nosed bats
    glide with erections
        and ejaculate
        just from the sheer joy of flight.
No doubt boy bushbabies circlejerk
    in the lightninglight
        as a ritual.
No doubt boy mandrills get erections
    watching boy mandrills get erections.
No doubt pubescent lemurs compare
    erection sizes in astonishment.
No doubt tumescent boy chinchillas
    make cute little comecries
        when they're jerked off.
No doubt boy badger boners are proud
    under the starry summernightsky.
No doubt boywolfdongs are just as much fun
    to boywolves
        as boyslothdongs to boysloths.

No doubt erect boyhyenapenis jumps
        when boyhyenas earlobes nibbled.
No doubt boy leopard phalluses
        are miraculous to boy leopards
            as they see them emerge
        all shiny and huge.
No doubt the horny pronghorn's prong
        is as velvet as his velvet horns.
No doubt armadillo lad's secret boylove
        moonlight rendezvous.
No doubt homosexual heroworship among
        orange-rumped agouti.
The jaguar cock exists.
The virgin jaguar boycock
        that gets erect in boyjaguarsleep
            and can spurt boyjaguar semen six feet
        soon will glory in ensheathement
            in girljaguar vagina.
Now boyjaguar jag off.

Robin Wayne Bailey
Ecce Homo

In candlelight, I watch you on my bed,
strange eyes half-closed, legs so coyly spread.
Dark valleys, shadows on your skin,
Muscled ridges conspire to draw me in.

Warm oil gleaming on my hand,
I straddle a bare butt—the holy land.
Annoint your flesh with a wise man's gift—
Slick fingers drift toward a dark and musky rift.

One digit—two!—massage takes on new meaning.
You lift your head and moan, a sensual keening.
My jealous cock swells huge and hard as brass,
A throbbing spike to crucify your ass.

I sprawl on top of you, hot to fuck—
You stop, look up, and whisper, "fifty bucks."

Robin Wayne Bailey
Thanksgiving

I was too poor this year
to buy a turkey
so I checked one out
at the bar, instead,
took him home, stuffed him good,
bound him, skewered him proper,
basted him with lots of butter
until ol' Tom was well done,
indeed,
if I do say so myself.

Leg and thigh, back and breast,
a nibble on the neck—
I ate him all.
(I do know how to cook!)

Still, it left me feeling
somewhat on the empty side
'til I remembered all
those starving Chinese children.
"Be thankful for what you've got,"
my mama used to say.
"Those poor kids would give
a lot
for what you've had to eat."

Well, mama always did know best.

Robin Wayne Bailey
Jack

Hot breath in my face
hands that move at the
speed of light,
you search my body
for sex.

It's been a long time,
you say, between the buttons.
I see it has;
your shirt takes off
like a rocket.

Laughing, I think
I like you.
Your grin shoots off
around my cock
and it's over

quick, like this poem.

David Bergman
Upon Julian's Clothes

Whenas in suedes my Julian flaps
Then, then, me thinks how snuggly straps
The rugged waistband of his chaps.

Next when I cast mine hand and feel
the skin-tight denim, hip to heal,
I'm glad I'm gagged and cannot squeal.

David Bergman
A Passionate Daddy to His Love

Come leave with me and be my love
And we will all the pleasures test
That circulate, they say, among
Thick arms, lips, legs, hard cock and breast.

And I will buy you shots of bourbon,
Blended scotches, rounds of Buds,
Sheets of satin, belts of leather
'Crusted o'er with metal studs,

Rub your back with scented unguents,
'Till your tense resistance falls,
Kiss your closed-shut lips and eyelids,
Bite your nipples, lick your balls.

You will moan with grateful sufferance
As tides of pleasure through you roll,
Giddy as my tongue explores
The inmost secrets of your hole.

I will shave your buttocks hairless,
Have you ride my cock all night,
Sweat will stream like stars grown porous
With a salty liquid light.

Then your thickened pearl-gray gism
Will shoot up through the steamy air,
Splattering my chest and stomach
And drip across my face and hair.

Exhausted we will rest together,
In one another's arms will lie,
'Til the break of dawn incites us
To acts we never dared to try.

So I'll ask you once and only:
Are these joys you're dreaming of?
If they are, then I'm your Daddy—
come live with me and be my love.

Dick Bettis
Encounter

Any perception of who I was disappeared
as, too, did my cock.
He would have swallowed all of me if he could,
never knowing who I was or if he should.

Dick Bettis
Metaphor

A sparrow sat on my cock
the other day
staying until it hardened.
I shot my load
and, happy, the sparrow flew away.

Mark Bibbins
Empire Video

PLAY

skin always looks warmer
when it's on television,
when it's just beyond reach.

PAUSE

the purplish head of a cock
poised in front of a man's mouth,
his full lips barely parted,
like he is whispering to it.

STOP

one winter, alone on grey afternoons,
i worked at Empire Video, often waiting
hours between customers. i furtively
smoked pot and watched pornos.

PLAY

it's better when they don't
look directly into the camera.
i don't want them to know i'm here.

PAUSE

a thin filament of cum,
heavier at one end, hanging
in midair, as though caught
in a spider's web.

STOP

i couldn't bring myself to jerk off
in the store, so i took the VCR back
to my apartment, hurrying through
the muffled streets with it like a date.

PLAY

my balls, tight and insistent,
are aching in my boxers
for these luminous strangers.

STOP

EJECT

Mark Bibbins
from a sky like this

along the placid, meandering road,
fog was forming above the fields
of milkweed, cowslip and thistle
in gauzy patches in the summer
    twilit night.
we talked as we drove up the mountain,
and you told me that sometimes you just
didn't understand women. you turned
up the stereo, smiled me an odd smile,
    and we were silent.
i stretched my arm out the window, ladling
the cooling night we rushed through.
i felt the wind fill my cupped palm
and imagined that this pressure felt like
    parts of you.
when the car sped up, the breeze turned
into a solid thing in my hand, and i imagined
that this might be how your bare shoulder
would feel as i pulled you gently
    toward me.
when we slowed down, the July air
filled my palm with a subtle weight
that i thought might be like your balls,
if i could hold them, resting in their
    bag of skin.
but i already knew such fantasies were
pointless, and that i should stop staring
at your tanned legs, lightly fleeced with

soft-looking blond hairs, or i'd end up
          walking home.
we climbed to the lookout atop the mountain
and i wondered if you saw the irony
in a straight man bringing his gay friend
to a place where the local boys took
          their girlfriends
to make out. probably not. we sat alone
on a low stone wall under the winking
stars, the concrete still warm under our legs.
below us, the tiny lights of our home town
          looked up drowsily.
you said, "do you remember, when we were kids,
how we used to lay in the grass and watch
the stars? sometimes, it seemed like
anything we wished for could come from
          a sky like this."
i felt like saying, well, almost anything,
but instead i leaned back and said
softly to the Pleiades: "yeah." there are
some things that even twenty years
          of wishing
couldn't have prepared me for. the feeling
of your fingertips quivering, as they brushed
silently on my thigh, was one of them. i felt
like i had swallowed an egg, shell and all,
          like a snake.
i didn't believe this could ever happen,
but you reached up and placed your hand
lightly on my cheek and pulled me
into a trembling kiss that made me forget
          about the stars.

our careful tongues glided together
and our hands moved eagerly over one
another's bodies, as we slipped slowly down
into the grass between the stone wall
    and the cliff edge.
your nipples hardened between my fingers
when they drifted under your tank top
and you whispered something that i
couldn't hear. our shorts came down
    to our ankles
and you swiveled around above me, on all fours,
and lowered yourself into the warmth
of my mouth, as you took me into yours.
we stayed like that, rocking slowly,
    for a long time.
the tastes of us later mingled in our mouths
when you laid on top of me, kissing me again
as you ground your hips into mine, our cocks
sliding together like two seals frolicking
    in the water.
i invoked all i had ever learned about waiting
so we could come simultaneously, and when we did,
the stars blurred and the sound of crickets
was lost to the soft groans that we couldn't
    keep from making.
after a while, we slid apart, damp with dew
and sweat and come. we dried off shyly
with paper towels from your car, then drove in
silence back into the twinkling valley,
    where we would
pretend we were the same simple boys
who used to ride bicycles through the woods—

who could never have summoned the nerve
required to do such things as those we had
    just done.

Walta Borawski
Surprising Kisses

For Malcolm

You were my first S&M man, you
showed me the ropes, though we
had to imagine them, in the dorm
at the St. Mark's Baths.

> *Don't move*
> *one wrist from the other, you*
> *ordered. Now lick me all over.*

And like a tired
or drunken ballet dancer my tongue
twirled, passion without form,
taking your pleasure moans for
applause, & flowers.

Now & then
I'd *plié* at your closed
mouth, lick your clipped beard &
tight lips;
now & then, on cues
very much your own you'd
open your mouth, & give mine
surprising kisses: How odd,
how more desirable these
than those given freely,
in uncategorized love, as if kisses

are just commodities, obeying
the law of supply & demand.

                    Later you
worried that my hair, wet all the while
from whirlpool & sauna, steambath & love-
sweat, would catch me cold. You offered me
taxi fare home. Surprising concern,
surprising kisses: But like men of
less choreographed fantasy you
said *Goodbye, & Good knowing you,* & I

danced uptown unbound.

Walta Borawski
Hunger

Paralyzed in heat
the man stroking
his cock does not
see the toilet door
is open, or men
entering, not
entering; he
dream-strokes:
he's needing
a hole to
come in, a
hole beyond
his fingers but

doors open, doors
close: hasty
steps, none
toward him.

The man is not *my type*.
He is no pirate. He is
no hippyhunk, bearded
& bandanna-ed. He is not
a hard hat on his lunch
break. He is not well-
contoured, there is no
color come-on in his
clothes. I go to my

knees before him, he
does not notice until
contact, wet lips
wake him, partly,

& he comes, giving
in, giving his
extraordinary
hunger to me.

William Bory
Ejaculation

Johnny can't read.

Oh! Faithful Johnny,
      let your store of fresh semen
      stream on these white pages,
   and, in cloudy gusts, embroider
      this dark piece of mine.

Let your heart, proof against ciphers and signs,
      alight like a swan
   on this black pool of worry.

Oh! How, in your wide bed, at night,
   John, you swim toward your dreams,
      as the sheets break around you,
   and the moon scrawls on your thighs
      her wordless poem.

William Bory
On a Subway Pick-up

Your clothes were wrong,
    or so they said.
You took them off,
    we went to bed,
    and there, your body,
        like a light,
made everything around it bright
        with beauty.

"He's such a clod.
    He's not too smart."
But you with lips
    and tongue and heart,
    when shades were drawn
        and lamps were out,
    said all the things I'd heard about
        in dreams.

"Where do you find these guys?"
        they said,
But I was cool,
    I kept my head.
    It wouldn't do
        to let them know
that there are angels here below
        the pavements.

William Bory
The Danger Zone

Your face is smeared on the pillow,
    slick with gooey kisses,
        as, gloating,
I chew your ass through your underwear.

Unspeakable,
    your butt, high and rosy,
    that cleft, deeper than thought,
        makes my flesh tremble
        on the bone,
    and, at night, when,
        with a wrench,
        we accomplish delight,
            I groan,
    as shades chatter and the moon
            is rapt.

O twice condemned,
    bitter treasure,
    you still rule this zone,
        below the belt,
    heavy with the smell of ball
                and bone,
    where, insolent and raving,
        we fall upon each other,
    where, askew, we hobnob
        till dawn.

Jonxavier Bradshaw
Answered Prayers

Prayers that are answered here
Are never heard in churches
What a place for a man to be

Once in the confessional
The priest questioned me
About reality
All I know is this
If you can't be touched like this
You can never understand
You can never be free
Really—

Exhaling a jock whispers loud
Fuck me
As he carries me over the finish line
While an executive in a three piece and tie
Rims my ass with a good wet tongue
It's hot all over today

This is a sanctuary of a different kind
I know the prayer circle front and back

I told the priest to get fucked
And he did
Much later
Experience that special agony
Crucified on the toilet door

He sure was surprised how fast
The gates of Heaven opened up
All in a moment
Forever

Eric Brandt
Sex on the East River

High tide, low tide,
In and out,
The East River flows.
Tankers unload
And rise.
The Domino Sugar plant
Up in lights.
Rounded towers empty now—
Only a sweet residue
Sticking to your skin.
The Williamsburg Bridge,
Twin pylons stretching their cables
To touch.
A constant state of arousal,
Of erection,
The crossing cars,
Small eddies of sperm.
Manhattan is fucking Brooklyn.

Perry Brass
For Old Men Who Suck Cock

What a blessing from nature
they are on our shore,
like rain past a five-week drought,
or a good Disney movie
when you're stuck with the kids
for a week in a seaside resort.

They remember our world
in a simpler way,
but rarely remember our names.
Or the games, or the gaffes
or the funny refrains
of the grudges we sip on in bars.

We find them alone
when the sun sinks down
and the wind suddenly whips up.
You go back to their rooms
and take off your clothes,
full of grit in the shivering dark.
Then fumble; smile;
make jokes for a while
and realize—while coming—
you're both seventeen again.

Perry Brass
Riding Around in Cars With Boys

How much fun it is riding around
in cars with boys—I still feel
that way today, probably since

I hate to drive, and they get such
a kick out of it—boys and cars
going together like icing and cake, and I

don't have to think about anything,
just riding around in cars with boys, and
it's always summer and salty and clean:

that sweaty, young sweat in cars with boys,
and the boys smell of English Leather
and lots of Jade East and other Kool-Aid

colognes they wear, and they have
such pretty faces and bodies with no waists
and soft smooth chests and downy arms,

and tight little baskets under loose pants
or madras bermudas or ripped cut-offs,
and they get in the car and we ride around

and they don't talk, but say everything
just by looking at you, and you know
they're curious and want to know stuff

about man-dick, getting nuzzled, licked
and laid; sucked; kissed all over—sweetly
fucked—they want to know all about that

but generally stay too shy to ask,
so the most they can do is be in the car
till you turn around and gently say

"Where you wanna go?" and they shrug
and say they don't know, and soon
it rains. Quick. Loud. And fast.

A summer night, with a wash-hard rain
and the car AC on super-blast, and they
say they're cold; and you slide over

to the backseat with them, and warm
them up with your mouth and arms;
and they're scared first to kiss you

but usually do, and their mouths
taste of Kool-Aid and their teeth
of heaven—light—shining in all directions;

and their peckers are so crisp and neat,
and poke out like little circus animals,
with small jeweled balls attached,

and they gush gobs of ivory cream,
and tell you they're sorry for squirting
on your vinyl seats—and then they want

to try you. "Gee, what's it like?"
they say, and then: "Don't tell
no one," and you know you won't,

because as nice as this time
always is, all you really want to do
is ride around in cars with boys.

Perry Brass
Wet Pink

I have eaten your sugar-cock
to become sweet
and your iron-cock
to be strong; still you pull

away from me, and allow me not
the wine of blood
from your pectorals.
I am too hungry you say,
and gallop off on your clickety horse,

but I know you will be back.
You are joined to me.
And even fear, sharp and bad,
head-wringing fear, even dog-fear,
will not keep you away
from my deep mouth.

Perry Brass
Men Are Showing Their Nipples
All Over New York

for David Swisher

It is July and men are starting
to show their nipples all over New York.
They are wearing skimpy little tank tops
with strings for straps—all scooped-in and low,

that look sexier even than all-out barechests
and they know it and they eye each other covertly
and men with dark pouty nipples
on dark Latin chests
look at men with pink, hairy nipples
on strong Nordic breasts
and they all think about nipples
and they all get hard and their nipples get hard,

and they smile and look at each other
and they want to lick and suck and kiss nipples,
but don't on the subways or the hot streets
but do in the bars and the loud clubs and we
find this charming and immensely
stimulating in the summer in New York.

Perry Brass
Cocksucking Aphorisms

In a more civilized world,
cocksucking would be declared
a more advanced form of kissing.

Very few men will ever remember
the exact way that the first three men
they ever went to bed with looked.
But who can *ever* forget
the very first time
a man sucked his cock?

There are very few things
certified "straight" men will always do
in the dark: one of them is simply
put your cock in his mouth,
if you don't ask him to kiss you.

Imagine how much happier
the world would truly be
if guys walked up to strangers
and offered to suck their dicks,
instead of coming up with
all the tired, sick, inane
boring ice-breakers
they usually maintain
they must resort to.

James Broughton
"Take good care of your dangle"

Take good care of your dangle
Raise your dangle with care
Pay him tender attention
Take pride in the way he grows

See that he meets the right people
and gets regular daily workouts
Give him every opportunity
to make the most out of life

With just a touch of encouragement
he can rise to sublime occasions
So take good care of your dangle
and dangle will take care of you

Regie Cabico
Art in Architecture

          Could
        Frank Lloyd
      Wright   create
    better structure
        what   lies
        between my
        lover & me
        is   where
        the similar
        transcends
        the   seven
        wonders of
        the   world
      Twin Towers in white
    sheets how his slopes
  against my teeth— a mini
skyscraper resting on a muscle
  boy rocks a   cultivated
    landscape   falling
      l i k e   Babel

Rafael Campo
The Passive Voice

Imagine why a man likes being fucked.
Imagine how my cock likes being sucked.
Imagine making love to me, my friend.

In English class, my teacher told us not
To use the passive voice; "It's weak," he said.
There was an older man who sometimes knocked

At my back door; I'd think of him in bed
And wonder if he'd like to make it break.
Imagine making love to him, my friend,

Until your mother finds your door unlocked.
Imagine what it's like slowly to bend
Beneath another man's gigantic cock—

The pleasures of the asshole aren't discerned
By many English teachers (mine was like
The handsome man I'd like to love instead)—

Imagine telling him. Of course, he's shocked,
But after several weeks, a note he sends:
"Imagine why a man likes being fucked,"

It says, and inexplicably so sad,
"Imagine how my cock likes being sucked."
In high school, no one seems to understand

This kind of love. It could be called dumb luck
Or disappointment, what happened in his bed;
Imagining why men like being fucked,

After his gentle, upright cock, I spent
The night in tears. Wrapped in his arms, I rocked.
Imagine making love to me, my friend.
Imagine why a man likes being fucked.

Marsh Cassady
A Cock a Day

"Wouldn't it be wonderful,"
my friend said,
"if cum
were a universal cure-all?"

Suppose you awaken,
at two a.m., guts in a turmoil.
You call your doctor
who advises: "Take two cocks
with a glass of water
and call me in the morning."

You feel lousy, are certain you
have a fever.
Toss that thermometer,
call a fuck buddy,
insert his dick in your ass.
Any dick will do, but why not
go for the best—long, thick,
veined and engorged?
Wait one minute, withdraw dick
and examine.
Red means fever.
If you have a fever
(or even if you don't),
reinsert dick,
fuck for ten minutes
and you're cured.

Pneumonia? The mustard
plaster's passé.
Ask a friend to sit on your chest.
Suck friend's cock to moment
of climax. Have him shoot
on your chest.
Rub in semen, collarbone to navel.
Several applications
may be necessary.

Listen to your doctor:
exercise, drink
plenty of liquids
and suck two dicks
before each meal.

Forget the wonder drugs;
dicks restore vitality,
cure heart ailments, get rid
of unsightly acne and prevent
baldness.

And always remember,
a few ounces of prevention—
in the form of a dick—
is proven more effective
than all the goddamn orange juice
you can drink.

Steven Cordova
JP

Dark haired and European, the fold
of his uncut cock was sometimes fragrant.

You are taller, blond, but speak
with the same, thick accent.

Is it between your long legs
that I want to plant my lips,

or in that country of Romantics
and Symbolists where I have never been?

Alfred Corn
Hot to Trot

Not so fast!—Emily Dickinson

Your body moves and touches me,
But—could you cool the pace?
We're headed for a photo finish
The first heat in the race.

Races are meant for track stars, right?
Or those who fuck to breed.
Me, I'd rather thrills and spills
Came at a lazy speed.

If music sets love's ideal tempo,
Let's spin a slow LP.
At 45, time might seem short,
But we are 33.

Our candle's burning at both ends,
The room's a bit too bright.
If you'd just trim the wick, big guy,
We could go on all night.

Peter Daniels
The Mormons in Sicily

There's something I didn't mention, that time we stood in
       the bus going to Monreale
watching the Mormons, noticing their badges—the title
       Elder translated "Anziano":
Anziano Norton, Anziano Schmitz, Anziano Miller, and
       Anziano Bellini the local boy,
returning from Utah with his brethren to convert the rest
       of the island,
perhaps including his mother. There was great zeal to
       labour in the vineyard.

What I didn't say was: as the bus filled with people and
       jolted uphill to the cathedral,
a man, crowded in behind me, was jolting in a rhythm that
       wasn't the bouncing suspension
and for a good ten minutes was fucking me, without
       actually fucking me, till the bus
came to his ordinary street and he got off as usual,
       while we stayed on
to the end of the line, to enjoy the Norman masterpiece,
       with the Latter-Day Saints.

Peter Daniels
The Valentine Gift

There's a Valentine gift in my trousers,
zippered up in respectable serge;
I've offered it sometimes to browsers
who have shown an appropriate urge;
underneath, it's wrapped up in white cotton
with elastic that clings to my waist;
and it could be a thing you'll get hot on
if it answers your personal taste.

I've a Valentine gift to delight you,
an expandable present that grows;
it has violet veins to excite you
as it opens its bud like a rose.
When you hold it, you'll cause a sensation,
for it's warmly responsive to thrills;
it will celebrate with a libation
of the fragrant white nectar it spills.

There's a Valentine gift I'll deliver
when I get to your far distant land;
meanwhile it brings joy to the giver,
being squeezed in the palm of my hand.
And for now, from across the Atlantic,
we can join in a rhythm for two:
start softly—work harder—get frantic—
and your gift will be coming for you.

Gavin Geoffrey Dillard
"Sex is something sacred and"

Sex is something sacred and
Profound, I said,

No, sex is something vulgar and
Profane, he said, wrapping

Four sweaty fingers and a
Thumb around my nuts;

You're right, I said,
Let's fuck.

Gavin Geoffrey Dillard
Jonah

I looked for a penis as big as myself. To throw my arms
around that vast rubber neck, to bury my face within his
somber yawning slit, smirking salivating glans. To feel
those vasculous throbs pulsing against my chest and
   thighs,
those veins as thick as my arms, impassioned with the
   lava
of life. I wanted something to be hanged upon, something to
burst my seams, to flay me and leave me desireless for
   more.
I wanted a lust I could not measure, that would never tire
or falter, an eternal saturnalia, that even when limp
   would
play whale to my Jonah. I wanted God and I found only
names and pamphlets. And this little stitch to put in my
mouth, and blow on, like a balloon that, once inflated,
   might
carry me to Heaven.

The Shroud of Turin never
held such mystery as this
rag of blue denim on the
bedroom floor;

The sloughed-off shins from a
reptile just skinned,
limp, yet crisp with
history:

> Stench of smoke from a
> disco dive,
> rhythm, fire and
> spilt beer;

> Stains of urine, sav'ry
> salts, the
> fertile seam of his
> rear.

He comes out of the shower,
slick and clean, a
serpent returned to his
lair;

But he is too late, my
heart lies spent, his
jeans now beside me are
there:

Dreams like dirty underwear;

Sperm on my gun.

He smiles at this treason;

Levi's: 501.

Gavin Geoffrey Dillard
"I would like to"

I would like to
shave your body clean

Strip its hair
to nakedness

See you bland
as a cave lizard

Shimmering, blind
as a white cave fish

If I might,
to touch your fleshiness

And move about
your glassiness

My lips
of pinkened steel

Gavin Geoffrey Dillard
"Twice a week Raymond and I would"

Twice a week Raymond and I would
attend the baths
he would watch me work out with
weights until I felt
full and desirable
then I would ask him to show me his
favorite man and I would
introduce myself to
that one
the three of us would share a room
and I would prove myself while
Ray looked on
when we returned home I would
make Ray's breakfast and we'd
nap before crawling out to our
wall on the street
I'd ask Raymond if he loved me
and he'd just smile like a mother who is
patient with her child

Gavin Geoffrey Dillard
"For a time I slept with both of"

For a time I slept with both of
them, always in the
middle
Steve would curl into me, cover me with his
great arms
nuzzle a moustache to the back of
my neck
Al would pat me and turn away, afraid to
show affection, burrowing a bare
bottom into my heated
lap

All three of us were porno stars
but they were lovers
for nine years they had been
married
we never quite had sex, the
three of us
they were far more attractive than
I
they were brilliant, but I
a genius
they are aging now
I am immortal
they have separated and Steve has found a
new lover
Al is studying something in the
mountains

And me?
I'm writing poems about
them,
always in the middle

Mark Doty
To Cavafy

We were talking about desire,
how sometimes only an image,
a surface compels us:
that boy, for instance, we watched
from the shore, standing with his back
half-turned to us out on the little raft

on Pond Number 10. Five divers—
characters in a story
I am inventing as much as remembering—
had paused on the raft,
in the air beginning to haze,
five o'clock light, the end

of August. Though they are only
a few feet apart, the distance
between them is carefully kept;
two study the water,
one looks away to the bank's
vague border. On the left,

the tallest are standing, high-school boys:
one faces toward us, arms
folded across his chest, taciturn,
shadowed, but light catches
his splendid friend's
wet shoulders and makes of them

a white bar in the misting afternoon.
It is almost too late to be swimming.
The gleaming one stands so surely,
legs spread just enough apart,
perhaps rocking back and forth a little.
What was only a remembered surface—

light on a boy's shoulders—
acquires depth, becomes nearly three-dimensional
as it is reconstructed;
I can sense, if not quite see,
the pond water streaming down
his shoulders. Is it solipsism

to love not the world
but what you make of it?
Or is that what we mean when we say
"memorable"—that we take something
from the surface of things and make it
ours? For him I might imagine

any present, any history, but what I see
are the loose green trunks he wears,
ones he's probably had for years,
he wears them so effortlessly.
The green water whitens his skin.
I think now his chest and arms

are becoming a little cool.
He and his companion are talking
and not talking, a low, laconic conversation,
without substance. As he is now,

really, since he is a memory reinvented,
and in the way of the stories we make

for ourselves out of whatever strikes us,
whatever makes us need stories,
something should happen. Nothing did;
he never knew we were watching.
I swam to the raft, waved to you
on the shore, slipped back into the water.

Of course we wanted him,
but more than that—we have
each other's bodies, better
because they are familiar.

We wanted to enter the way
he dove unselfconsciously

from the little dock,
certain; the diver
becomes pure form, the exact shape
for parting water. I think had there
been a single question in his head
he would have disappeared,

or have been someone else,
and I think, imagining him,
of Cavafy, of encounters in upstairs rooms
recollected in upstairs rooms.
His must have been a life upstairs,
remembering what happened over there,

beside the washstand, where the blind
would edit half the bed
with its dark crosshatching.
Someone he met on a streetcar,
over a counter of handkerchiefs,
someone he could remember.

For a little while their caps
would hang on a hook beside the door,
those men so fleeting in body—
a train to catch, an appointment—
becoming more mute and ideal,
more permanent as they were revised.

Had his hand passed right through them—
the iris-blue vein in a chiseled arm,
a thick, dusky wrist—I don't know
that it would have mattered. I don't know
that he ever really wanted to touch anyone.

David Eberly
Phone Sex

from a twenty-three year old:
am I alone? am I hard?
He introduces himself—Tom.
Three o'clock in the afternoon.
He says he is stripped down
and hot for sex. I see him
young, smooth, oiled up,
his cut cock wet as he lies
stretched out on his bed,
calling and calling until
he connects, just like that.
He asks me to describe myself:
weight, height, size, age,
the usual characteristics.
Something clicks:

        we start
to talk as we lie side by side
like the lovers we both lost.
Our hands move over our chests
as we whisper what we want,
urgent to touch. Do this,
do that—the phone cord wraps
itself tighter around my legs
while we jack off. Then
he says he's done and hangs up.

Edward Field
Dirty Old Man: Two Variations

1.

When I go senile, I swear I'm going to let go
and grope everything in sight—
the Italian waiter in his black trousers,
that soulful-eyed hasid at the discount store,
the doctor leaning close to take my blood—
what I've had to hold back on all my life.

So what if they put me away
in a nursing home?
I'll feel up the attendants,
who may well think,
Why not let him? Don't do me no harm.

2.

For once in my life
I'm going to be free
and grope everything in sight:
Let them cut off my hands, palms
still hairy from adolescent onanistic bouts,
I'll grope with my toes—
they'll have to amputate them one by one.
Then my tongue, my lips, my toothless gums.

Let them take away part after part,
something forbidden is still possible
with kneecaps, elbows, ears—
every part of me has a dirty mind.
And through it all I'll stare my fill
right up to when they seal my eyes.

They can cut out my heart, of course,
but even that's no guarantee:
My newly-liberated senile ghost
will go a-roving day and night.
And then what's to stop me groping
every man in sight?

Edward Field
Rockabilly

I wanna be your jockey shorts
that hold your cock and balls,
I wanna be your underwear
and be there when it falls,
releasing all the bounty of
your bouncy genitals.

I want to cup your downy cheeks,
squeeze between, and sniff and taste,
and run my elastic band like greedy
fingers round your waist...

I wanna be your jockey shorts
that hold your cock and balls,
I wanna be your underwear
and be there when it falls,
and watch you shaking out
your soft and bouncy genitals.

And when you slip your hand in,
I'll caress you fore and aft,
feeling your foreskin sliding
up and down the shaft...

I wanna be your jockey shorts
that hold your cock and balls,
I wanna be your underwear
and be there when it falls

in a heap to the ground in worship of
your bouncy genitals.

And when it rises throbbing
against my cotton knit,
I'll stretch and let it fill me up,
and when it shoots, drink all of it...

I wanna be your jockey shorts
that hold your cock and balls,
I wanna be your underwear
and be there when it falls
all in a sweaty heap beneath
your juicy genitals.

Edward Field
The Moving Man

He was a burly, curly-blond ape of a man
who had a moving van
and a bunch of young helpers he paid by the job.
He treated those boys like a harem,
picking one for his pleasure when he wanted.
He had wrestled them all to defeat
for when they fell under his weight
with that huge body on them
they went dreamy as desire took them.

Having him for an example, they were a rowdy gang
hanging around the office at the front of the garage,
waiting for a job to be called in.
They kept wrestling and grabbing at each other
with an eye cocked for the boss's approval,
half-teasing him with their slim bodies,
muscled from work.
The van stood behind in the shadows
with its tailgate down, empty
except for the quilts they wrapped furniture in,
lying in a heap.

In the idleness of the afternoon
the boss would start horsing around with a boy,
perhaps one who had been especially fresh,
and chasing him through the dark garage
force him right up the tailgate into the van.
There they fell rolling on the quilts

until the man, pinning him with his chest,
pulled down the boy's pants—
his own were always open.
Large hand roved down naked belly
to the clutch of hair and hard-standing prick,
with balls a handful,
and the boy yelped, but had to stay.

His wrestler arms tamed that young body like an animal:
Holding him prisoner, he forced him over,
his cock probing the backs of his thighs,
the cheeks of his ass. One hand on a breast
fingered the nipple, the other arm
pulled him closer below
with a hot, demanding push.
He breathed hard on the plum of a cheek,
and bit at the boy's neck,
his stubble scratching as he growled in the boy's ear,
teaching him pleasure.

Now he held in his arms the whole boy,
his fat prick nosing between those round tight cheeks,
until the boy, completely submerged in that loving hulk of
a man,
relaxed with a moan and opened,
and the moving man moved his prick all the way in,
taking his sweet time.

Edward Field
His Finest Hour

It's bigger than he is, I heard,
as I woke up in the barracks,
one hot Sunday morning
in Texas.

Several soldiers
were standing around my bunk
where I was lying
naked on my back,
on the verge
of a wet dream,
cock rock hard
and pulsing.

Hey! I yelled,
and pulled the sheet up just in time,
as the guys walked away,
grinning.

Allen Ginsberg
Please Master

Please master can I touch your cheek
please master can I kneel at your feet
please master can I loosen your blue pants
please master can I gaze at your golden haired belly
please master can I gently take down your shorts
please master can I have your thighs bare to my eyes
please master can I take off my clothes below your chair
please master can I kiss your ankles and soul
please master can I touch lips to your hard muscle
    hairless thigh
please master can I lay my ear pressed to your stomach
please master can I wrap my arms around your white ass
please master can I lick your groin curled with blond soft
    fur
please master can I touch my tongue to your rosy asshole
please master may I pass my face to your balls,
please master, please look into my eyes,
please master order me down on the floor,
please master tell me to lick your thick shaft
please master put your rough hands on my bald hairy
    skull
please master press my mouth to your prick-heart
please master press my face into your belly, pull me slowly
    strong thumbed
till your dumb hardness fills my throat to the base
till I swallow & taste your delicate flesh-hot prick barrel
    veined Please
Master push my shoulders away and stare in my eye, &

make me bend over the table

please master grab my thighs and lift my ass to your waist

please master your hand's rough stroke of my neck your palm down my backside

please master push me up, my feet on chairs, till my hole feels the breath of your spit and your thumb stroke

please master make me say Please Master Fuck me now Please

Master grease my balls and hairmouth with sweet vaselines

please master stroke your shaft with white creams

please master touch your cock head to my wrinkled self-hole

please master push it in gently, your elbows enwrapped round my breast

your arms passing down to my belly, my penis you touch w/ your fingers

please master shove it in me a little, a little, a little,

please master sink your droor thing down my behind

& please master make me wiggle my rear to eat up the prick trunk

till my asshalfs cuddle your thighs, my back bent over,

till I'm alone sticking out, your sword stuck throbbing in me

please master pull out and slowly roll into the bottom

please master lunge it again, and withdraw to the tip

please please master fuck me again with your self, please fuck me Please

Master drive down till it hurts me the softness the

Softness please master make love to my ass, give body to center, & fuck me for good like a girl,

tenderly clasp me please master I take me to thee,

& drive in my belly your selfsame sweet heat-rood

you fingered in solitude Denver or Brooklyn or fucked in
a maiden in Paris carlots
please master drive me thy vehicle, body of love dops,
sweat fuck
body of tenderness, Give me your dog fuck faster
please master make me go moan on the table
Go moan O please master do fuck me like that
in your rhythm thrill-plunge & pull-back-bounce & push
down
till I loosen my asshole a dog on the table yelping with
terror delight to be loved
Please master call me a dog, an ass beast, a wet asshole,
& fuck me more violent, my eyes hid with your palms
round my skull
& plunge down in a brutal hard lash thru soft drip-fish
& throb thru five seconds to spurt out your semen heat
over & over, bamming it in while I cry out your name I do
love you please Master.

May 1968

Allen Ginsberg
Come All Ye Brave Boys

Come all you young men that proudly display
Your torsos to the Sun on upper Broadway
Come sweet hearties so mighty with girls
So lithe and naked to kiss their gold curls
Come beautiful boys with breasts bright gold
Lie down in bed with me ere ye grow old,
Take down your blue jeans, we'll have some raw fun
Lie down on your bellies I'll fuck your soft bun.

Come heroic half naked young studs
That drive automobiles through vaginal blood
Come thin breasted boys and fat muscled kids
With sturdy cocks you deal out green lids
Turn over spread your strong legs like a lass
I'll show you the thrill to be jived up the ass
Come sweet delicate strong minded men
I'll take you thru graveyards & kiss you again

You'll die in your life, wake up in my arms
Sobbing and bugging & showing your charms
Come strong darlings tough children hard boys
Transformed with new tenderness, taught new joys
We'll lie embrac'd in full moonlight till dawn
Whiteness shows sky high over the wet lawn
Lay yr head on my shoulder kiss my lined brow
& belly to belly kiss my neck now

Yeah come on tight assed & strong cocked young fools
& shove up my belly your hard tender tools,
Suck my dick, lick my arm pit and breast
Lie back & sigh in the dawn for a rest,
Come in my arms, groan your sweet will
Come again in my mouth, lie silent & still,
Let me come in your butt, hold my head on your leg,
Let's come together, & tremble & beg.

Boulder, August 25, 1975, 4 P.M.

Allen Ginsberg and Peter Hale
Violent Collaborations

Violate me
in violet times
the vilest way that you know
Ruin me
Ravage me
utterly savage me
on me no mercy bestow
                    —OLD SONG, 1944

Trespass against me
& penetrate deeply
Spare me not even your rape
Tie me up quickly
Make me smile sickly
Seal up my mouth with scotch tape
                    —AG

Piss on me Crap on me
Wipe your fat ass on me
Make me a creature you loathe
Sorely harass me
Don't even ask me
But deal me your ultimate blow
                    —PH

Ignore me & stomp on me
Crack your big whip on me
Make me get down on my knees

Order me to suck your dick
Spank me & do it quick
Shove it in deep as you please
           —AG & PH

Stun me & shun me
Slave me & shave me
Give me your loathsome disease
Fuck me & fist me
In your army enlist me
Poop on me when you're at ease
           —AG & PH

Degrade & debase me
In public deface me
Come on my beard in the mud
Double me over in summertime clover
Then hose me down w/your stud
           —AG & PH

June 1992

Thom Gunn
Hedonism

After the Scythians, how advance
In the pursuit of happiness?
They went around in leather pants,
And every night smoked cannabis.

Thom Gunn
The Problem

Close to the top
Of an encrusted dark
Converted brownstone West of Central Park
(For this was 1961),
In his room that
            a narrow hutch
Was sliced from some once-cavernous flat,
Where now a window took a whole wall up
And tints were bleached-out by the sun
of many a summer day,
We lay
    upon his hard thin bed.

He seemed all body, such
As normally you couldn't touch,
Reckless and rough,
One of Boss Cupid's red-
              haired errand boys
Who couldn't get there fast enough.
Almost like fighting…
We forgot about the noise,
But feeling turned so self-delighting
That hurry soon gave way
To give-and-take,
Till each contested, for the other's sake,
To end up not in winning and defeat
But in a draw.

Meanwhile beyond the aureate hair
I saw
A scrap of blackboard with its groove for chalk,
Nailed to a strip of lath
That had half-broken through,
The problem drafted there
                 still incomplete.
After, I found out in the talk
Companion to a cigarette,
That he, turning the problem over yet
In his disorderly and ordered head,
Attended graduate school to teach
And study math,
            his true
Passion cyphered in chalk beyond my reach.

Thom Gunn
Saturday Night

I prowl the labyrinthine corridors
    And have a sense of being underground
As in a mine…dim light, the many floors,
    The bays, the heat, the tape's explosive sound.
People still entering, though it is 3 a.m.,
    Stripping at lockers and, with a towel tied round,
Stepping out hot for love or stratagem,
    Pausing at thresholds (wonder never ends),
Peering at others, as others peer at them
    Like people in shelters searching for their friends
Among the group come newest from the street.
    And in each room a different scene attends:
Friends by the bedful lounging on one sheet,
    Playing cards, smoking, while the drugs come on,
Or watching the foot-traffic on the beat,
    Ready for every fresh phenomenon.
This was the Barracks, this the divine rage
    In 1975, that time is gone.
All here, of any looks, of any age,
    Will get whatever they are looking for,
Or something close, the rapture they engage
    Renewable each night.
                  If, furthermore,
Our Dionysian experiment
    To build a city never dared before
Dies without reaching to its full extent,
    At least in the endeavor we translate
Our common ecstasy to a brief ascent

Of the complete, grasped, paradisal state
Against the wisdom pointing us away.

What hopeless hopefulness. I watch, I wait—
The embraces slip, and nothing seems to stay
    In our community of the carnal heart.
Some lose conviction in mid-arc of play,
    Their skin turns numb, they dress and will depart:
The perfect body, lingering on goodbyes,
    Cannot find strength now for another start.
Dealers move in, and murmuring advertise
    Drugs from each doorway with a business frown.
Mattresses lose their springs. Beds crack, capsize,
    And spill their occupants on the floor to drown.
Walls darken with the mold, or is it rash?
    At length the baths catch fire and then burn down,
And blackened beams dam up the bays of ash.

Thom Gunn
Nights With the Speed Bros.

Lovers, not brothers, whatever they might say
That brilliant first night, being equally blond,
Equally catlike as they reached beyond
The tropes of dalliance to the meat of play.

What I still keep from our long lamp-lit climb
Through gallant and uncertain fantasy
Are marginal gaps a window granted me,
When I removed myself from time to time.

I gazed at moonrise over the wide streets,
A movie letting out, a crowd's dilations,
Bars, clocks, the moon ironic at her stations:
By these the window paragraphed our feats.

Then dawn developed in the room, but old.
…I thought (unmitigated restlessness
Clawing its itch): "I gave up sleep for this?"
Brown leaf replaced the secret life of gold.

Trebor Healey
We Started Out Janitors

and ended up fuckbuddies
He used to mop the floors without a word
while I vacuumed couches and dusted tables

I figured he didn't speak English
We both figured the other was straight
We started out janitors
now I clean his asshole with my tongue

It was a restaurant
We both started stealing food from the fridge
big sausages and blocks of cheese
We started laughing one day when a cube of butter
dropped out of his pants
as we were locking up to leave
We laughed so fucking hard
and then he said "I hate this job—
let's take everything and not come back tomorrow"
We started out janitors now we're thieves

He said his boyfriend liked pastries as he bagged 3 dozen
blintzes
I said I'm queer too
He said the only thing he liked more than food was sex
I said you wanna fuck?
He turned and forced his tongue in my mouth hard
We tore at each other's clothes
We both had big ugly dicks
that we treated like food

We started out janitors
and now we were sucking cock on the kitchen floor
He fucked me as I held the back of a chair
and I came onto his mopped floor
We laughed some more and took all the food

We both showed up the next day
I guess to find each other
took everything and came back
They didn't fire us
They didn't even notice
We stayed working there for 2 more months
fucking like crazy and cleaning less and less
We started out janitors
now we're fucking-connoisseurs in a high class restaurant

We both got fired in the end
for doing a lousy job
but what did they know
We were investors
We started out janitors
now we're unemployed fuckbuddies with something better
to do

Trebor Healey
Hustler

He had a versateller card for a cock
He'd insert it into horny old men with money
He knew all the right buttons to push
and he'd thrust his beautiful credit
in over and over again
pumpin' his payback
while the machine groaned
and made those chirping sounds
like a bird
$20 for every thrust
bang bang bang
and the twenties would pop out like blackheads
bang bang bang
like a slot machine
He was a one-organed bandit
And he laughed when he saw the oranges
and the apples line up in rows in the old man's eyes

Scott Hightower
Finding Love

There were clothes freshly cast off,
some positioning
    and counter positioning
in the car—encapped by white cliffs;
    quite a place
    to find love
after having found
outside a full moon shattered in the river.

There was a white leg, my leg,
in the shadow of the car—
    raised up—
that came down—into the moonlight:
    quite an awful gesture.
    Made us
gasp our breaths
like Icarus in the water.

Scott Hightower
In Medias Res

I am already inside. But the dumb
fingers of each of my hands probe your armpits
as if looking for an orifice. My tongue
and lips have found one

of your feet; already know what to do with
it...and it's toes. Tomorrow I must remember
to give you the word for it, "shrimping." Be
but foresworn...thyself.

Reach in beyond all ironies, all violence,
all panics. Feel the black wind on everything
beneath your naked face. Feel the water
lifting you up. Open.

Unlock. Believe in your own presence,
a lotus blooming like a syllable inside
your dark lungs. Let craft and passenger and
wind all groan as one.

Richard Howard
"Richard, May I Ask a Horrible Question? Isn't It Painful When Two Men Make Love Together?"

There is a horrible answer, to part of it—when
two men make love apart, that is the most painful.
Remember what I say—it may come up again.
  But you mean something else:
bodies whose engineering has failed to manage
or match their architecture, in which case Power
gets no good out of Form, or only the better
  of Form. Is that what you mean?
There is a solution (*I* mean, it is soluble):
you concentrate upon the parts and let the whole
take care of itself. Anyway, what about pain?
  Is there pain and not-pain?
Or is there the discovery that they become
each other when you traverse a certain terrain?
It is like electricity, pain: not a thing
  but the way things behave.
Behaving yourself, then, is a way of having
yourself be; pain a manner (sometimes a Grand one),
not what is the matter. Merely signifying,
  it is significant.

Richard Howard
The Snake-swallower

He was quite a young man, and, judging from his face,
there was nothing that could account for his having taken
up so strange an occupation. He was very simple in his
talk and manner. He readily confessed that the idea did
not originate with him, and prided himself only on being
the second to take it up. He said he saw nothing disgusting
in it and spoke of the snake in general as a reptile capable
of affection, not unpleasant to the eye, and very cleanly in
his habits.

—Mayhew's *London Labor and the Poor* (1851)

The snakes I use are not so long
    As you'd expect for show.
I try to find them thick enough
    To make the going slow,
Not slick. And always hold a pair
    Aside: you never know.
I keep them warm in flannel rags
    Or straw, but even so
The winter shrivels them to string
    After the first snow.

Straight off, and I was just a boy
    Before I started in,
They tasted queer: sticky, tart
    But sweetish too, like tin
When you bite on a knife. They draw
    The edge of your tongue thin,
And the roof of your mouth comes over rough
    When the slippery skin

Slides. It helps to get there first
    With a finger of gin.

The scales may scratch your pipe a bit
    (Not so it gets scarred)
When you pull him back again.
    A snake, see, moving toward
Ever so small a hole is like
    Water being poured:
Smooth all the one way. Mind,
    Don't show him you're scared,
Else he'll turn to a proper gag,
    Stiff as any sword.

The head goes down about an inch
    And the rest of him all
Continues in the mouth, curled round.
    I hold him by the tail
And when I pinch, he goes in smart.
    If you let him, he'd sail
Right down; mostly, though, they stop
    After a two-inch crawl
Down the swallow; then they bind
    In the mouth like a ball.

I was only the second that did it
    Ever. The first you know
As well as me: our First Mother on
    A night off, that's true.
It's nothing to do with what you like,
    It's what you're used to:

I know a man bites the heads off
    Chickens for *his* brew.
It isn't much different, what I do,
    Except it's what I do.

Eve now, like I say, when she
    Took to the habit
Of swallowing, the courtly round
    Came quick to love it,
And don't they say, besides, somewhere
    That Christ came of it?
These days in the country, though,
    When you do it clever,
They swear you're the Devil Himself,
    And they won't have it.

Abraham Katzman
Public Service Announcement

It's 3AM. Do you know
where your dick is?
It's 3AM. Have you hugged
your dick today?

Abraham Katzman
Wicked Child

I want you blindfolded by a tallis.
I want tallis clips on your tits.
I want the leather tefillin cord tight around
the base of your cock. I want the same
cord binding your wrists behind you.
I want it to hurt some.
I want you to be blond,
a blond jew, loose curls. I want you
standing before me holy and loved.
I want you floating peacefully on my bed
as if on Dead Sea saltwater,
held up by the density.

I want you speaking to me,
telling me what your body feels,
reporting to me like you are
exploring a cave, exploring the
cave of yourself. I want to
observe. I want to see.

I want your tits now.
I tug on the chain holding
the tallis clips together.
I tug harder until the clips
snap free of your body.
I lay the chain over your shoulder,
tell you not to let it fall.
I want to twist your nipples.

I twist them. I want your tits
confused. The chain slides off.
I don't hear it hit the wood floor.

You are in the desert now.
You are wandering as my
hand finds your cock.
I press my palm to your chest
as I pull your cock toward me.
You arch your back some.
Your cock is all you are for a moment.
I lead you to my bed,
untie your wrists,
wrap the leather cord
around the length of your cock,
the prayer box close to the head.
I want your hands on me.
We build a sukkah together
on this bed, three walls, no roof.
I will fuck you this way.
Never let you cum.
Never let you cum.
I want you to feel your ejaculation
with your ass. I want you to
feel it inside. I want you to
talk to me as you cum. I want
your ass to talk to me. You will
cum with my dick in you.
My dick will hear you cum,
fighting the leather cord
that binds your cock,
sheaths your cock.

I'll unblindfold you then,
show you your cum then.
You will cry at the hours passed
in this desert, at the years passed
in this desert. You will cry
when I show you your jewcum
and I will explain to you the wicked child.
I will explain to you this holiday.
I will explain to you Passover.
How our people, our tribe, wandered the desert
for forty years. How we were slaves in Egypt.
How our gay tribe of jews
fucked each other's asses
even then in the dessert.
How we spoke of it as holy.
As a way to understand G-d.
As a way to understand.
In the desert our brown skin,
our cum on brown skin.

I will explain to you,
on this holiday of our togetherness,
how I was once a wicked child.
How wicked children grow to be
wicked men. How I am selfish.
How I love myself. I want the tallis
pressed to your face now.
I want to see the outline of
understanding on your face.

I want your skullcap off.
I want to see your hair.
Your jewcum on your belly.
Your safety in being with me.
Your loving being with me.
Your yiddishkeit
unmistakable as you finally cum
and are still surprised.
As you cry at the beauty of your cum.
We are men. We love each
other. We are jewish men.
We love each other.
I love you most.

Your cum in my palm
as I show it to you.
I am showing you the child,
the baby we have created.
And it is a wicked child
as we are wicked. You smile
and are beautiful.
You cry and are beautiful.
You are beautiful.
It is a wicked child.

Dennis Kelly
Edward Field

While meeting a young man
at a street fair
with a baby
in his backpack,
reach down and squeeze
the proud young father's cock,
asking him casually,
"Got any extra babypaste
for an old queen, kido?"
While meeting a young jogger
in the park some fine afternoon,
slip down his shorts,
untangle his warm cock
from his jockstrap
and give it a good tug or two.
While shopping
some day in Safeway,
corner the grocery boy
in the frozen food section
and crudely reveal
to all just how much smegma
the kid has underneath his delicate apron.
Another time,
take a cuteboy at the vets,
lean him up against the barking dog cages
and fasten your lips to him
like a sticky, famished,
distraught Venus flytrap.

Wherever you are,
be there
and be ready
for some nice
unthought of
love-
action.

Dennis Kelly
A Big Blue One

His pale hippie manroot
has a long tuberous vein running down
the length of it—a big blue one.
It drains the tiny delicate tributaries
of his nice smooth foreskin,
forking out at the tip into dozens of
cocky capillaries and archipelagos of desire.
Thick and exquisitely flat up along his hard stomach,
his erection is the most elegantly lethal thing I've ever seen.
So streamlined and smooth, so exquisitely vulgar tasting.
His still somewhat unjaded RFD innocence
makes his climax even more excruciating,
because his cock is so far from
being innocent-looking and innocent-acting.
Even when it's flaccid and shrunken up
tightly after a swim in the pond,
there's still something captivatingly
chthonic about his young prairie cock.
Over the several years we're lovers,
I get to know the in's and out's
of his thick virile manroot pretty well.
I love him so much I'd just as soon suck the snot
out of his pug-nosed, enflared nostrils
as I would sperm from his big fat Kansas cock.
During the winter months both his nose
and his pretty prairie prick
ooze a lot: salty pearl jam stuff.
Ropes of it—thick as toothpaste,
thick as snot

Dennis Kelly
What if After So Many Blowjobs

And what if after so many blowjobs,
the cock itself doesn't survive?
What if after so many erections,
the hardon stops? Quits for good?
It would no longer get to be
swallowed, played with, fondled
in long restless moments.

To have loved at least ten inches,
to impale oneself on lanky organs,
carried away with love of chicken,
gay abandon in the darkness of
boyish pubes, shadowed by the
moment when orgasm looms overhead.

What if after so many gay poems,
I still don't get to know him,
seduced by simple things like
money or Cadillacs, barging into
lonely steambaths, what if I
forget later, out of the blue,
the length of his love for me.
or combing my hair, what if I
look in the mirror & see an
aging stranger, will I be
swallowed up by it, eaten alive?

There's a lot to say for cameras,
hiding the grief which words know,
looking our of eyes that are a
lens. saying nothing about joy
or its escaping us, forgetting
the way he talked in bed after
sex or was anything said at all?

Ja

"Handsome blond bearded Aryan
type 30, 170, 6'1" seeks intro to gay
S/M scene, singles or group. Pic
appreciated. Box 7444"

—a *Boston Phoenix* personal ad
May 22, 1973

1. Anon.

I was myself looking for
an intro into the S/M
    scene about a year ago,
and I thought I would offer you

    what I found. Since an old friend
had mentioned a Boston bar named
    The Shed on Huntington Ave.,
I started there. My impressions

    of the Shed were as follows:
the action, which doesn't pick up
    until around ten p.m.,
is at its best on Friday and

    Saturday nights. It's the kind
of impersonal place you can
    spend an entire evening
without a word from anyone

if they don't know you. I sensed
the presence of two distinct groups:
        leather guys and a second
group that likes to be around them.

        I got to know a waiter
pretty well. He told me there were
        probably only four or
five genuine S/Ms who came

        into the place. Most of the
leather types struck me as girlish—
        referring to each other
by women's names, for example.

        I stopped going to the Shed,
at any rate, after a guy
        who works for me walked in the
door. Now I confine myself to

        a large and congenial gay
crowd (no S/M) on the North Shore.
        Well, I've gone on long enough.
Hope you find what you're looking for.

2. Jim

I am a white male, twenty-
eight years old and masculine, who
    is into the S/M scene,
having found it capable of

    providing pleasurable
experiences. It's also
    a most stimulating way
to live out some fantasies with

    others. Perhaps you will find
this happening to you. I have
    learned to be careful, about
contacting people, however,

    and prefer to relate with
others who also feel this way.
    I have found that these people
turn out to be the ones with whom

    you can communicate and
the ones who will take the time and
    effort to develop those
scenes which will increase each other's

    satisfaction. This also
tends to eliminate those who
    are not sane or clean since they
are too impulsive to go in

for some mutual screening.
I suppose that you are also
        interested in screening,
since you requested a photo.

Of course I appreciate
your reasons for requesting a
        photo, but I would never
send a picture blind to an ad.

You can appreciate my
reluctance to comply, I hope.
        Have you any questions to
ask of me? Feel free to do so.

3. Ted

I still read the *Phoenix* ads
although I decided a while
    ago to stop answering
them. The problem was that no one

    I met through them described him-
self as he was. You, however,
    sound sincere, so I'll give it
another try. I'm twenty-six,

    six feet, weigh one seventy-
five; I have brown hair. blue eyes. a
    good body; I'm considered
handsome and masculine. I've been

    involved in the S + M
scene for about five years, but not
    exclusively, as there are
many worthwhile people who don't

    dig that scene. I enjoy it
a great deal, however, and have
    several friends who enjoy
it as well. You mention a "group"

    introduction in your ad,
but—may I be impertinent?—
    would warn against that sort
of initial introduction

unless you are going with
someone you know. It could get a
bit sticky. I don't see much
point in going here into my

sexual preferences
as I am fairly versatile
and have no idea what you
are looking for in terms of an

introduction. I have been
honest in describing myself.
If you have as well, give me
a call I'm in after seven.

4. Bill

I read your *Phoenix* ad and
must admit to being intrigued
   by it. Although it doesn't
tell too much about you, it said

   just enough to arouse my
curiosity. Since I don't
   have any pictures of my-
self to send you, let me describe:

   I am in my thirties, five
foot nine, one hundred and sixty
   pounds, fairly well built, almost
pure blood German (a little of

   something else on my mother's
side), blue eyes, light brown hair, mustache.
   I really dig leather—and
have leather jeans, chaps, jackets, boots,

   cap, etcetera, as well as
a suitcase full of leather and
   chain toys—belts, paddles, a cat
o' nine tails, etcetera. It sounds

   as if you might be new to
the scene (or is it just new to
   the Boston area?), but
if you are interested in

finding out more about the
possibilities, contact me
     between nine and five, Monday
to Friday. Also: do you have

     leather—and what; do you have
any other gear—toys, leather
     or not; what is your scene; what
would you like to do and what

     role would you play? My cellar
is available between the
     hours of nine and five, and when
I'm high enough anything goes.

5. Larry

I just finished reading your
ad in the *Phoenix* and found it
        interesting enough to
respond to. I'm a gay white male,

        thirty-eight years old, five foot
nine tall, weighing one hundred and
        sixty pounds, and am very
interested in welcoming

        you into the S/M scene.
I've been gay since I was sixteen
        years old and lived with a guy
for three and a half years in a

        slave-master relationship—
he the master, with me being
        the slave. Everything he asked
me to do—from tying his shoe

        laces to licking his boots
I did. There were weekends when I
        would be greeted at the door
with my supper in a doggy

        bowl—after I had come
from work on a Friday—and not
        been permitted to get up
again until Monday morning.

I would like to have that kind
of relationship again with
    the right person. I enjoy being
in bondage and being

    disciplined by someone who
digs the idea of having a
    slave. If you think you might be
interested, give me a call—

    I'm home most evenings after
seven. P.S. If you were the
    guy with the badge on at the
Shed on Saturday night, then WOW!

6. Len

Read your ad in paper.
I am new myself to gay world—
    would like to intro to it.
So I am interested in

    getting together with you.
Maybe it would be good if we
    intro each other! I am
willing. What do you say? Are you?

    I am in the U.S. Coast
Guard—I am thirty-three years old—
    straight all my life—now find that
I like to look at other guys—

    get turned on when I see a
goodlooking pair and cock. I am
    back from Nam—been two months with
nothing—real hot and horny now

    for some action. Must act soon
or a wet dream will ruin
    everything. Haven't had it
up for six weeks—urge to jerk off

    but then that's kid stuff. So let's
get together—enjoy intro
    each other into gay life!
I am stationed in Sandwich—

on canal. No phone, so please
ride down to East End—find station—
    you will see rest room in front—
park car—open trunk—I will be

    waiting and come down. I get
through on Thursday this week early
    (May 28). Try to be
there for two o'clock. That gives me

    time to clean up and shower.
Meet this hot sexy jock—and share
    as only two men can the
full joy of coming together!

7. Marvin

Found your ad in the *Phoenix*
to be a decided turn-on,
    but you didn't say what your
interest was: S or M. I

    like to dominate (I can
be real mean—or very gentle).
    What I like best is turning
an ass red-hot, with either a

    belt or the palm of my hand,
but there are many other joys
    to be had: work with hand cuffs,
ropes, dominance submission games.

    I see by your description
of yourself, you are bigger than
    me (I'm five feet, ten inches,
a hundred and forty-five pounds,

    I have shortish dark hair, green
eyes, I'm twenty-seven years old
    and well hung—but I *can* be
tough.) Write and tell me what you

    dig (or think you'd dig). Also
enclose a *fuller* physical
    description of yourself (am
very interested in things

like body hair, ass, etcetera).
You sound promising: please answer
        quickly. Are you German or
Austrian? You say you're thirty.

        That would place your birth—in this
country or abroad?—in forty-
        two or three. Was your father
or any of your relatives

        involved in the second World
War? Do you have Nazi helmets
        or uniforms? As my name
suggests, I'm Jewish. Pic enclosed.

8. Hank

My name is Hank. I am just
twenty-seven years old I am
    very good-looking I am
masculine I have a very

    good body I am well hung
I am clean I have a nice pair
    of balls I have long hair, not
to long I am butch acting an

    appearing Let me show you
an teach you about gay sex, plus
    introduce you to the S
+ M scene The places to go

    The things to wear I know how
to do things that will drive you wild
    in sex I will make you feel
so good. I all so have wild an

    sexie friends. That we can have
sex with. They are in their twenties.
    They are good looking. They have
big dicks. They are masculine. Me,

    I don't dig fems I don't dig
fats. I just like a good looking
    guy that is straight appearing
an has a nice size dick, long an

fat. Call seven four two-six
three three two an leave a message
   for Hank. That's me. Leave your name
an your number. I will call you

   back. Call on this date Sunday
May thirtieth between three to
   nine in the evening. Tell
me the size of your dick. Are you

   straight appearing? When you set
your eyes on me you will dig me.
   Let me show you a good time.
I am what you are looking for.

9. Rudy

Aryan, indeed! The word shuts
down thought, whatever its effect
    on fantasy, which in your
case, apparently, was racing

    out of control. Your need to
establish your membership in
    the Master Race—was that on
account of your having failed to

    measure up in any race
of your own, to become master
    of an identity, for
example? Well, *Heil* there, Miss Thing;

    no, I will not chide you for
trying to scare up worshippers
    of your blond beast persona
in lieu of loving yourself, which

    could not be counted upon—
particularly inasmuch as
    I remember you found no
one to…dig (no letter, at least.

    to answer) from among the
twenty-five that your help-me-rise-
    again-from-ashes *Phoenix*
ad elicited—though you kept

them all as signposts—along
the road not taken *yet?* Had you
sensed—it is my message to
you across the years—that we do

not lack for mentors in the
sadomasochism of daily
life? that whether or not you—
I—become involved in S/M,

we always are: life provides
(we provide each other with) all
the introductions to pain and
pleasure we will ever need.

Victor King
Shackled Nap

You just lie there
all cozy under me you
don't have to do a thing
I'm not going to hurt you
no no just going to start
your cute little butt burning
split you good right in there

Sorry about having to
gag your pretty mouth
but it's just as well
because it gives me this
chance to talk to you now
without your mumbled boy-
banter parrying at my arms

You just relax and
grip that bed let's
not bruise your wrists
You just relax while
I heat up the big one
that's right baby you
just squirm under daddy

Thinks of it as massage this
exploration of your boy buns
you just lie there with your
pretty jaw clenched fingering

the mattress with your nipples
oh this is just a little warm-up
the real moist ache's yet to come

Come on boy reach for the nob
reach for it slicing your crack
make this old heated slab feel
your hungry ass begging for it
and don't start with the jerking
till you really mean it boy cause
you're gonna need it for this ride

Victor King
Valentine

I long for you
when I wander alone
not you talking or touching
just there following
in my space poised
attentive

Understand now that
I never condescend to
express anything sexual
unless you kneel at my feet
and smolder
untamed

Learn
to wait
for my velvet grapple
to present you posed and whimpering
and sieve your soul
through mine

They frighten me
the nights when I can't say no
the terminal access my soul offers
the bleeding lust to have
cock burn my belly

Those nights
of speeding sizzle-lows
my flesh dilated swollen with yearning
sledge-hammering my temples and brow
with blood and significance

Victor King
A Little Addicted

Your cock glistens from my belly,
salutes my glance. And inside.
Oh, inside, my little satyr,
tongues, my pet, tongues
press into each other,
press into your
hardness.

Between my legs the lust bulge cries for you,
reaches for you, begs for your meat
to cleave my aching anguish away.
Hot-seared pleasures plunge
wild and wanton
into my heart.

Come, oh come, my love,
fuck me lust-laughing
into squirming bliss.
Flood me. Sperm-
swirl me into
ecstasy.

And finally,
finally,
rest.

Victor King
Mother of Invention

The men were shackled each night
to the barred wall
at the foot of their beds
as they stood on their benches.
It was lowered, rotated down
until each lay spread-eagled
braced to the bunk.
Cries of the new inmates
those not accustomed to this constricture
and the pissed sheets
and the occasional
shredded clothing in the morning
rang through the night
for weeks on end.

The men would stand
in their ankle-hobbled
crucifixes
on their benches
locked in the clamps
for the roll to be called
and the "ride"
they all laughed about
during Recreation.
Then the bell would ring
and amid hoots and hollers
modern technology
would lower them
to their nightly bondage.

The prison was then "open"
exquisitely freedom-teasing.
The cleaning crew came in
throughout the night
their work boots stepping
through the "windows"
their mops swabbing
the toilets
then the floors.
Then of course Ian Cilobaid
who founded the facility
would peruse the premises
late into the night
hooded.

Wayne Koestenbaum
Erotic Collectibles: 1977

This is how I learned
arts of suction, how stars
and comets of ancient sway
fumbled for preeminence

in my still adolescent body:
at the library
I interrupted *Paradise Lost*
to use the lavatory.

Hole between the stalls afforded
a view of my first man:
the archetypal divinity
student. We walked

through unearthly foliage
to his neo-Bauhaus
fascist-era dorm.
Down went our pants.

He had only one ball.
What happened to the other,
ghost ball? I stayed
until dawn, came home with guy taste

in my mouth, wondered
if my straight bunkbed mate
would sense my new
uncomely fellatio aura.

Was I aglow?
Was I visibly fallen?
This night had been
necessity, not pastime.

Burning, I revisited the trick
one numinous evening.
"I've got spring fever," I said,
justifying perversion

with the comforting old saw.
I wore Lee overalls.
Swashbuckler, he undid them.
"Enfold me, Satan," I thought.

By day I snubbed him;
only at night could I admit
I wanted to lie
naked and hoovered in his bed.

He had no extra flesh;
I remember his Irish
spareness. Now
you may be dead, my ethereal

initiator, you who led me
through foliage.
Each gesture was an accident.
No mythic embroidery

surrounded us, only
the story I am telling now:

the last time I saw you
I was drifting in cowboy boots

through the immense white
mystery of Garden Street,
my Bartók score
within a gloved hand,

sun against the already
fallen snow so unnaturally bright
I thought I was walking
toward catharsis—
my trio rehearsal at the block's end.

Wayne Koestenbaum
Erotic Collectibles: 1978

He worked at a gas station,
or wore a gas station
jersey—or I blew him
near a gas station.

I said, "Can we go to your
apartment?" He said no
with sudden terrified solemnity,
as if it were taboo

to confuse tea-room and home sex.
I crammed this blow
job into my busy schedule
because my shrink had said,

"Have as much sex as you want,"
so by God I'd better
take the prescription and wake
my listless "Lycidas"-

reading body! How did I find
my way into his stall,
and did he welcome
my brash entrance, did he growl

"Hey there, foxy"? Dingy
light poured onto my clean,
hypothetical groin.
For ten syrupy minutes

he was the man in my life.
He waited for me, he didn't
pack up his dick and leave
the premises the minute he came.

Courteous, he understood
laws of reciprocity
that govern even the most
casual encounters.

What is casual? I did not feel
casual. My heart beat
fast, as if this were an audition.
After the event, I walked

down Revere Street, past
his gas station, or, if I
am imagining his connection
to gas stations,

then I can't justify why I associate his
mouth and its accompaniments
with a still-life Mobil sign
at trolley's end, where the sea

resumes its fabled nearness to the sand.

Wayne Koestenbaum
Erotic Collectibles: 1992

One man's dick had the quaint
malleability of Gumby—
and a Cheops eminence.
It was a private

theatrical. I smiled
at the melodramatically
self-exposing man and he
smiled back—intimacy

via mirrors in the men's room!
I'd made a friend
amid the dream's bulrushes!
There was no temporality,

no progression, no drama:
only teeming, succulent sight.
The proffered dick
in question was, naturally,

my childhood friend's: Dougie's.
It had the same hotdog quiescence,
the same look of threat.
Meat-colored, it stiffened—

a revolutionary
Gorgon or papyrus, veined
and brought out of pants
with a sense of surprise

attack and anti-climax.
So one acknowledged
the penis but also said goodbye
to it, ignored it, nourished

no reverence. These men
were postcards; they wore
an arty stillness.
My chest's short wiry hairs

never converged
to form a general picture.
My terse pectorals
had a breast look. In the hollow

between the mounds
a saint's medallion hung,
to ward off injury.
You understand that in the dream

I was a timorous youth,
no nimbleness informed
my sexual conduct.
Outside, time's cataract cascaded,

and the weird tiled eternity
of the basement, the dive,
continued, a travelogue
I can't transfigure.

This was my vision.
These were the exposures

that lit up my night.
I saw the naked men,

I was one of the troupe,
and now I am telling you
about their tendrils, anatomies, smiles.
My never-to-be-fathomed men come here

to unzip their pants
and show me their message,
their lullaby,
their ghost story—

whose haunted ending never shifts.

Michael Lassell
Personal foibles #1

I like to sleep with the smell
of a man's cock on my hands,
maybe the smell of cock and
lightly scented oil,
maybe the smell of my own
cock, maybe not, maybe
the cock of a Thai boy at the
Gaiety Burlesk (his hips
politely tilted at the last
moment to take my finger)
or a dark-skinned Caribbean
from the Show Palace:
uncut, semi-hard, hose-like,
dripping discount baby lotion—
I'm a perfectionist,
so I can't afford to be
fussy. Not just any
Tom dick or Harry cock will do,
but cock that has
lingered in my hands while
a stranger's eye fixes hard
on mine and doesn't know if
I want him to cum or if I'm
going to cut if off with a
razor hidden somewhere about
my nudity, a cock that
has smelled fear, or ambiguity
at least, a cock that went

looking for a hand with
cash in it and
found mine in
my pocket. The smell of
cock on my hands makes me
sleep soundly and dream
of beauty.

Michael Lassell
Nipples

So I happen to find
my tongue on his tit
that one time
and he lets out this sound
like I just stomped down
on an ingrown toe, only he's
got it muffled into his
throat so
no one will hear.
I try the other one, just so
his psyche won't be warped by
an asymmetrical encounter of the
sensual kind, and he says:
"Oh, baby,"
which is not
an ingenuous reply.
Perhaps he's been watching too much
cable TV.
"Suck me," he says: so I—
being literal minded—
slide down the rigid torso to his
nether belly, but he
pulls me back up
with the flats of his hands
over my ears like
muffs to crush a
skull between and
plants my mouth at

breast level.
"What is this," I think,
"some weird excursion into
Renaissance iconography?" But I
get the picture when he croons:
"Oh, God, this is good"
like some Guggenheim matron ogling the
Russian avant-garde for the first time.
"This guy's been reading too much
Adult Fiction," I think
as one nubby nugget
stiffens between
two rows of tender teeth.
Then it hits me like
an algebraic solution in the
nick of time that
some men have endings in
greater nervy quantity
in vicinities the
master mammary builder
forgot to erect on
my own corporeal winterscape
(throwing up igloos in lieu of
cathedrals), but
the colossal injustice of *that* is
harder to take than
cocks on a scale from
tee-hee-hee to
ho-ho-ho. He
picks my free hand up,
puts it on the other knob, and
teaches me to tweak like

I really mean it—I was
right about a-
symmetry.

And so it goes till sunrise,
him purring like a
Mercedes Royce,
responding like a logo cat to
precision control equipment.
All he can't do is
stop on a dime. I wonder
how hard I have to drive before
he shifts the abdominal gears and
lifts his knees up to his
chin hairs, but
I don't wonder long.
By dawn I'm
slick to death with axle grease,
expertise, and
envy—and he is
bumpers deep
in love.

Michael Lassell
Casey/jones

Casey gives nickel blow jobs
in the quarter peeps on Eighth off 42nd
to support his habits:
heroin, humiliation, and men.

Nights he seduces with eyes like
Dietrich's on the *Shanghai Express*,
muffler wrapped around his face
like a sultan's numero uno.

He's just in from Philly,
or so he says. Like as not
he'll be dead before New Year's:
If the drugs don't kill him
or the plague,
the druggists will
or John Q. Homo-erectus
with a steel-edged hard-on.

"You want me to use a rubber?"
I ask,
safe in the shark's tank,
but his mouth's already full.
His eyes say it's a new question and
way too real, man, way too real.
he keeps those mandibles working
without a word.

He knows
how to serve
and how
to get what he wants
and how
to make you think in passing
there's no one else on earth but you, babe,
no one but you.

His dick is small and soft,
his belly smooth and white like
Garbo in *Camille:*
flawless porcelain and doomed.

Who's using who?
Ask me later. He needs more
than me, and I need nothing at all
except him: Casey and his aching jones.

"I'm going to come," I say,
my body dripping sweat,
winter heat pounding in my head without
cracking into thought.
It's over
in no time.
In no time,
I'll want him again.

I hand him a ten for
good behavior.
He knows where to look a gift horse
and how
to look grateful

instead of ready to be sick.
He dresses with practiced aplomb.
His chaste kiss is
wet and
cold with semen.

"Usually I'm kind of wary about goin' anywhere,"
he says,
"but now I know you, okay?"
he says,
like we just signed a seven-year contract
with options,
his eyes like Marilyn's
when she goes back to drinking alone in
Some Like It Hot.

Days Casey watches at the
Show Palace threshold of
porn and panting,
vamping tricks form the streets like a pro-
fessional fisher of men.
Days he wears a conning rap
strung-out like pearls:
"There's some spiritual shit, some spiritual shit
goin' down in the basement,"

he says,

"in the basement of the hotel,
some satanic shit,
somethin' 'bout a dead baby
in the basement of the hotel,"

he says,

"and some woman jumped off the
twentieth floor,
I don't know, I seen her."

He asks me for quarters and
another waltz in his
two-by-two confessional booth, but he's
crazy now with eyes like
Swanson's in *Sunset Boulevard*,
reading for his closeup,
Mr. DeMillionaire,
and the poppy rot has
cut black spots into his teeth,
his lips are split and scarred,
and I was a fool
to touch him,
and he was a fool
to touch back,
and there we stand
on Eighth off 42nd,
two cool fools with a jones on
out to score some serum truth
to get us through another day of
bloodless ritual.

Michael Lassell
Imagining a peach

Think of a peach,
the largest you have seen,
sun-ripened, its blush from
tan to crimson covered
by a platinum down.

Split it in your mind,
extract the cratered pit;
hear the ripped seam of
parting flesh.

Peer into the hollow, its
walls a convoluted womb,
red as caves where virgins
once were sacrificed at first
bleeding; their rush of blood
gave rubies and peaches their
fervor.

You salivate touching your
lips to the moist perimeter,
sweeter than any fruit you've
ever tasted; probe deeper.

Harden your tongue, push;
burrow into the soft center.
The meat gives way, reshapes
itself around your language.

Your teeth break skin. The
peach surrenders its nectar.

Now tell me again that you
just do not understand us
homosexuals.

Michael Lassell
The going rate

The going rate is
40 bucks but
some of them will
do it for less weekdays.
Alberto did it for
30 because I was
"nice."

Tony said he'd go with me
for 20 but
Tony's got a dollar sign
cut into the hair at the
back of his head, and
Tony is not
Alberto, though
it was sweet of him
to offer.

In the back room
Alberto sips off his
clothes, then
mine. There is no
kissing, of course,
nothing that might
leave a mark on his
pride. Alberto's straight,
you see, or so he says.
Still, he's more direct

than most people you'll encounter
on a Thursday.

I come fast and apologize:
my semen gets
on his shoe.
"Part of the work," he says
with an accented grin and
wipes it off, then me.

If you want to
get off with Alberto
bring cash
and believe when he says
"I like you" that he's
never said it before
and won't again
before sunrise.

Michael Lassell
How to find love in an instant

Sit as close to the stage as possible.
Look like you're one of the kind who's buying and
like you've got the wherewithal.
Look into his eyes.
Look into his lap.
Covet him as loud as you can without speaking.
Do not touch. Just worship silently.

Applaud; show
appreciation. At the end of the set
let him approach you in the lounge where
Boys Meet Boys. He will put
one hand on your left tit and one on the
tight bundle of your jeans and
offer a private session for 40 bucks.
If you've got it, give it.
Don't dicker.

After you're both naked, he'll
rub his oiled body against yours.
You will be hard and hot and
grateful. He will be soft and bored
but attentive.

You will walk out into the night and no longer be
afraid of 42nd Street.
Now you are part of it
and the locals can tell.

You will smile to have been accepted
and descend the subway stairs
knowing yourself better than ever
and better than ever
thinking yourself just fine.

David Laurents
Stopping by the Glory Hole
on a Snowy Evening

Whose woodies these are I do not know
But all are ready for me to blow.
These men have made their way to here,
Though the roads fill up with snow,

And all are undeniably queer.
I could not do them all in a year!
My own cock begins to ache
With so much manflesh near.

One man gives his cock a shake
And there can be no mistake
He wants to thrust it deep
Within my throat as far as I can take.

These halls are lovely, dark and cheap
And I have promised myself
Miles to go down on before I sleep,
Miles to go down on before I sleep.

David Laurents
The Frog Prince

Lying naked atop the sheets in the summer heat
his lumpy genitals press against his crotch
like a frog crouched
in the thick reeds of his dark pubic hairs.

"Kiss me," they whisper,
"and I shall grow into a prince."

David Laurents
Traveler in Flight

As a kid I always got a hard-on
on the bus to school.
Then, embarrassed, I hid my excitement
to be going somewhere.
Now I masturbate on airplanes.
It doesn't matter if it's a business trip
or a vacation, the glamour of flight,
of being able to create a new persona
for the passengers and strangers I meet
turns me on. I lock myself in the lavatory
and sit upon the toilet, my legs spread wide
above the bowl, my cock arching up to meet
my hand. And as I stroke myself I flush,
again and again, to feel each time that chill
as the bottom drops out, the delicious cold air
of the outside sky, limitless and vast beneath me,
and the possibility that someone is looking
upwards.

David Laurents
Romance

so much depends
upon

a long court-
ship

glazed with
anticipation

beside the white
orgasms

Timothy Liu
The Size of It

I knew the length of an average penis
    was five to seven inches, a fact
I learned upstairs in the stacks marked 610
    or HQ, not down in the basement
where I knelt behind a toilet stall, waiting
    for eight and a half inches or more
to fill my mouth with a deeper truth. The heart
    grows smaller, like a cut rose drying
in the sun. Back then I was only fourteen,
    with four and three quarters inches
at full erection. I began equating
    Asian with inadequate, unable
to compete with others in the locker-room
    after an icy swim (a shrivelled
bud between my fingers as I tried to shake
    some semblance of life back into it).
Three times a day, I jacked off faithfully, yet
    nothing would enlarge my future, not
ads for vacuum pumps, nor ancient herbs. Other
    men had to compensate, one billion
Chinese measured against what? Some said my cock
    had a classical shape, and I longed
for the ruins of Greece. Others took it up
    the ass, reassuring in their way,
yet nothing helped me much on my knees at night
    praying one more inch would make me whole.

Timothy Liu
Reading Whitman in a Toilet Stall

A security-man who stood, arms crossed, outside
the men's room (making sure that no one lingered)
met my eyes with the same dispassionate gaze as
a woman inside, kneeling to clean the toilets.

The faintly buzzing flicker of fluorescent light
erased the contours of a place where strangers
openly parade their sex. Efficient, silent,
all ammonia and rubber gloves, she was in and

out of there in minutes, taking no notice
of the pocket Whitman that I leafed my way through
before the others arrived. *In paths untrodden, /
In the growth by margins of pondwaters, / Escaped*

from the light that exhibits itself—how those words
came flooding back to me while men began to take
their seats, glory holes the size of silver dollars
in the farthest stall where no adolescent went

unnoticed. O daguerrotyped Walt, your collar
unbuttoned, hat lopsided, hand on hip, your sex
never evading our view! how we are confined
by steel partitions, dates and initials carved

into the latest coat of paint, an old car key
the implement of our secret desires. *Wanted:
Uncut men with lots of cheese. No fats. No femmes.
Under twenty a real plus.* How each of us must

learn to decipher the erotic hieroglyphs
of our age, prayers on squares of one-ply paper
flushed daily down the john where women have knelt
in silence, where men with folded arms stand guard

while we go about our task, our tongues made holy
by licking each other's asshole clean, shock of sperm
warm in our mouths, white against the clothes we wear
as we walk out of our secrets into the world.

Timothy Liu
The Prodigal Son Writes Home

For Richard Howard

I want to tell you how he eats my ass
even in public places, father dear,
the elastic round my waist his finger hooks
as it eases down my crack (no classified
ad our local paper would run, I'm afraid,
            but that's just as well).
We met in a bar that's gay one night a week—
teenage boys in cages, men on the floor,
but that's not what you want to hear, is it?
how he noses into my cheeks on calloused knees,
lip-syncing to the rage of techno pop,
            that ecstasy of spit.

He's after me to shit into his hands.
What should I say? (I told him I'm afraid
he'd only smear it across my wide-eyed face,
hard as it is to tell you this.) How plans
have gone awry is more than apparent here—
            this sty he calls a home
tender as a mattress filled with our breath,
our sex unsafe. *Oh stay with me,* he croons,
my eyes clenched shut, head trying not to flinch
as he makes the sign of the cross on my chest
with a stream of steaming piss, asking me
            if we were born for this.

Michael Lowenthal
Inhibition

I wish I were not so decent,
did not have such goddamn good
judgment. I wish I did not see Jesus
bleeding for me every time
I want to do it.

Nothing would stop me
from picking up the boy who bags
groceries at the Stop & Shop, the one
with the mustache too wispy
to shave, skin stretched
so tight over his new-grown muscles that the veins
bulge out and every leg, every arm,
every part of him looks like a hard-on
ready to explode.

Nothing would stop me from befriending
the kid, buying him sodas, asking him
to my place to shoot
some hoops and after, when he's using
the shower, bursting in and pulling
the curtain. Nothing would stop
me from prying apart the vise
of his unseasoned buns and forcing a finger
inside, then two, then my cock.

But I was raised too well. I am too aware
of the issues around domination and abuse.

I am involved in a nurturing relationship
with a caring and good-looking man.

So I wheel my cart into aisle 14
instead, the aisle next to the one
where he's bagging. I don't even look
until after I've paid, when I catch
a glimpse of him balancing eggs
at the top of someone else's
bag, the back of his neck
sweaty in the bare fluorescent glow.

Michael Lowenthal
Witness

Of all the boys I jerked off
in front of, when that was the closest
I could get to sex, the one who sticks
out is not John, who let me come
on his stomach, or Danny with the pubescent
balls so suddenly huge he worried
they might be cancerous. The one who visits
my fantasies most often, who keeps me
company now that masturbation is again
the most viable option, is Leonard.
Skinny as a twist-tie, scrawny bowed legs,
with a hooked nose that couldn't keep
his glasses up, Leonard was not the man
of my dreams. But there was something
about his quiet curiosity, the squinty stare
he was always refocusing.

The day he came home with me
after school, we watched *M*A*S*H* reruns
in the dim family room. Hot Lips Houlihan paraded
her ample chest, teasing Leonard's eyes
wide as they ever stretched, the size of coin
slots in a pay telephone. "Size matters
for guys too," I pointed out, my dick already
poking past elastic. "Ever measured
to see how big you are?" Leonard shrank

away from me on the couch, pushed
the glasses to the bridge of his nose.
Freed from fabric, my dick snapped
out recklessly, a mousetrap
set off by the mere suggestion
of touch. My mother's sewing tape
revealed the proportions—not bad
for a fourteen-year-old. Then with practiced
technique and a touch of showmanship,
I tugged until white froth formed
between my fingers. Leonard watched, hot
breath so heavy it fogged his thick
corrective lenses.

He eventually let me measure him.
Not then, but a few days later. Skinny
as the rest of him, blue veins against palest
ivory, his dick seemed a fragile ornament,
the spout of an antique porcelain teapot.
But that's not what I think of when I think
of him, not the stiffness that became as familiar
in the next few weeks as my own. When I'm alone
at night, when the health aide has left and I
lie here wondering how anybody could look
at my emaciated frame, skeleton jabbing
through the ashen skin, and see anything
but a corpse-in-waiting, I remember Leonard's
eyes that inaugural afternoon. He tried to turn away
at first as if from sudden brightness, the flash
of an exploding bomb. Then he squinted,

refocused his gaze, and I saw shock
give way to curiosity. It was a look
of admiration and arousal, telling me
I was giving as much as taking in,
that in spite of himself Leonard wanted
to see everything. He wanted to witness
all of me.

John McFarland
At Home and Abroad

I had backyard sex with somebody from the gardeners
And the entire lawn was covered with seed.
I had toilet sex with somebody from the plumbers
And my pipe still leaks, though it's all stickied!
I had ordinary sex with somebody around the corner,
But I found myself, for once, blocking it.

I had animal sex with somebody from the zoo.
You're shocked, but tell the truth, wouldn't you?
I had regular sex with somebody from the Serutan
And, I mean twice a day, like clockwork, BAM!
I had weekend sex with somebody from the phone company,
And I was shocked the connection was so bad.

I had batty sex with somebody after *Dracula*
And it couldn't have been better hanging upside-down.
I had toe sex with somebody from the ballet.
What was the point, I completely forgot?…
When the sex at home completely loses its way,
It's time to pack a lunch and take a hike.

Once away, I had cowboy sex with somebody in a corral
And it was, if I may say, a lot more than just OK.
I had encyclopaedic sex with somebody from Brittanica.
We zipped from A to Z, but did the Index twice that day.
I had papal sex with somebody from ancient Rome.
Forgive me, Father, for we did sin, especially him.

I had bitter sex with somebody from a lemon grove.
The tang was fabulous, but the bite was nasty.
I had worthless sex with somebody from the World Bank,
But listen, you don't know what small change can be.
I had mano-a-mano sex with somebody from Pamplona,
And I know why the bulls always prefer to die.

I had really cheesy sex with somebody from Brie,
Then even greater sex with somebody from Gouda.
I had nutty sex with somebody who was a true escapee
And it was a riot, what with the funny jackets.
I had back-door Attic sex with somebody from Greece,
Oh, Venus, why does my penis draw me to these places?

I had gravy sex in Turkey, slippery sex in Iceland.
I went everywhere and did almost everybody,
Except in the Arctic and then Antarctica,
Where I didn't touch a soul. And when I came back
To my building, what do you suppose?
I had fantastic bi-polar sex
                right in the laundry room.

Rondo Mieczkowski
Thirteen Ways of Looking at a Penis

I

Among twenty cruise bars
The only throbbing thing
Was the head of the penis.

II

I was of three desires,
Like a crotch
In which there are three penises.

III

The penis shriveled in the autumn winds.
It was a smaller part of the landscape.

IV

A man and a man
Are one.
A man and a man and a penis
Are one.

V

I do not know which to prefer,
Sex in the morning
Or sex in the afternoon,
Ejaculation
Or just after.

VI

Men filled the narrow hallway
With barbaric flesh.
Lengthening penises
Crossed it, to and fro.
The longing
Spewed out of the shadows
An inexhaustible cause.

VII

O buffed boys of West Hollywood,
Why do you imagine golden dildos?
Do you not see how the penis
Stretches the 501s
Of the men about you?

VIII

I know *Honcho* and *Drummer*,
The Advocate, *Genre* and *OUT*;
But I know, too,
That the penis is involved
In what I know.

IX

When the penis flopped back into his pants
It marked its retreat
With a moist, expanding circle.

X

At the sight of penises
Pendulous in the moonlight,
Even the stand-and-stare queens
Would line up hungrily.

XI

He drove over California
In a Cabriolet.
Once, a fear pierced him,
In that he mistook
A shadow of a cloud
For his penis.

XII

The ass is shaking.
The penis must be rising.

XIII

We fucked all afternoon.
We fucked
And we were going to fuck.
The penis throbbed,
Ready once again.

Rondo Mieczkowski
This Is Just to Say

I have eaten out
your boyfriend

who was in
your bedroom

and who
you were probably
saving
for dessert

Forgive me
he was delicious
so hot
and so spicy

Edmund Miller
In the Porno Theater

Now suddenly everyone's hot to be
Tight with me. Why, I'm all aglow tonight!
At least I must be doing one thing right
Since sitting rub-a-dub snug beside me
Is a guy who's passed me up many times.
Yet he lunges for my little nipper,
Fingering my crotch, opening my zipper,
Hoisting me erect, setting off my chimes.

But all the while this expert boldly sucks,
I long for something worth the whole nine bucks
Paid at the door. At last I catch the eye
Of a better guy, eye-lashed, standing by.
Groping this hunk enables me to shoot,
But, then, I find *he* gives *my* hand the boot.

M. S. Montgomery
An Abstract of Baskets

The question, gentlemen, that I would pose
concerns the variations in men's crotches,
the age-old problem: does the build, or clothes,
produce them? Data, from a man who watches,
suggest that length and height of front crotch seams,
the style of zipper shields (or fly fronts), sorts
and quantities of fabrics, and extremes
of amplitude or stricture found in shorts
or pants contribute much. While width and height
of wearer's waist and hips, the volume of
the genitals and buttocks, and the sight
tumescence makes cannot be ranked above
the garment's cut, still, leotard or kilt,
much, too, depends on how the man is built.

M. S. Montgomery
The Wrestler

We'd done some testing, several times before
in practice, so it didn't much surprise
me when, while resting on his basement floor,
he said, "The Greeks all grappled naked. Guys
would grease each other up to make it hard
to get a grip."
      His courage shamed the fear
that grabbed me. "If you'd shuck that leotard
I bet I could! You got some goop down here?"

From ground position we tried cradles, locks,
reversals, scissors, a full body press
that juxtaposed and pinned our slippery cocks,
switching the combat into a caress,
showing us, when the equal match was done,
that in our stalemate somehow both had won.

M. S. Montgomery
On a Condom

Unboxed, this droll bizarrerie we share,
this frisbee some athletic elf might throw
or diaphragm Raggedy Ann might wear,
shows little promise that a man might grow
to like it; even less when it's unrolled:
like some dead, pallid, desiccated worm,
this shapeless rubber object, flat and cold,
seems wholly unerotic.
              I affirm,
however, dearest, when you put it on
and bring its honeyed hardness towards my face
or, waking warmly up at early dawn,
insert it gently in my dream's embrace,
I worship as a talismanic glove
this golden emblem of my lover's love.

Carl Morse
Free on Tuesday Nights

The beautiful statue in its niche
is perfectly willing to respond
to somebody's dreadful inner need.

The other best way to be assured
of participation in heightened form:
let every man on the stairwell know
with an unmistakably torrid glance
that you could be home in seconds in a cab
—or even swifter (ditching all this crap)
locked in the john on the second floor
swallowing each other's tongues.

This makes visiting the Whitney Museum
almost bearable.

Carl Morse
Brahms Never Sucked *My* Cock

Oh being asked if a certain famous co-star was gay,
Tallulah Bankhead snapped: "How should I know? He
never sucked my cock."

Brahms never sucked *my* cock,
but I truly believe he would have if he'd heard
my dream Sieglinde or my bird.
Then he'd have loved me for a lark
and tossed me breadcrumbs in the park
and stroked my pinions in the dark.

Then he'd have lured me to a shack
and run his damp nose down my back
and sniffed for motifs in my crack.
Or caught me jumping ship to shore,
my pee-pee jutting like an oar,
and penned a nautic overture.

Brahms' own cock was scored four-hand,
with whole-note balls thrown up on land.
He loved playing top-up concert grand,
and stretched the barriers of class
pretending to compose for brass
loose variations on the mass
by triple-tonguing navvy ass.

So what if he did have protégés, all male,
adored sopranos seriatim *à folie*,
and died at sixty-three without a wife,

having just burned his journals and his life.
He couldn't possibly have been gay.
He never sucked *my* cock. Oy veh!

Carl Morse
On Reading a Book of Poems
by Black Gay Men

for Assotto Saint

The coal-black love keeps leaping off the page
and sticking its pink tongue down my throat,
so I kiss all the spit-drenched vowels back,
deep-brain each thrusting noun and verb,
and take each rock-hard gerund up the ass,
boosting white literacy to an all-time high.

Christopher Murray
The F Train

Homage to Frank O'Hara

Fire on the subway tracks!
Sound the glorious alarm!
That homeboy stud is cruising me
on the F train from Brooklyn!
America, land of opportunity,
God bless your subway system,
sweet cars of desire still
playing possum with my heart.
Who'd have ever thought
that in these shiny, metallic
days, we'd be stopping at nothing
save romance and Jay Street/
Borough Hall, the crossroads
of my world and his? Stop me,
stop me! Who knows
where this might lead?
The wheels spark with passion,
the small windows rattle like
jealous voyeurs. The ride
is consumed by his quick,
licking looks that fog
me up so nice. Roll,
baby, roll. Don't stop
until we crash and burn
each other up, melting metal,
squaring wheel, until

there's nothing left, until
our empty ashes blow each other
out, playfully, slowly,
into the East River's
melding stinky mix
where we'll swim
out into some real
deep fucking shit
to kiss the algaed hem
of Our Lady Liberty's drag
in heartfelt horny thanks
for underground lust
and freedom.

Harold Norse
The Gluteus Maximus Poems

Ah, sir, what are you fondling so fondly
    under the spray? You think you're
    unobserved, but your half-hard belies
    the macho pose—and you, sir, there
    in a corner at your locker, twisting
    your rod from view under a towel,
    a stiff curved bow of anxious meat.
    And you in the steam room, glancing
    at soggy newsprint, black
    and beautiful, fighting down
    a rising tool, it's no use, sweetie,
    desire will out, don't hide, let go!
    No one recruited you, forced you
    to love those muscular buttocks,
    smooth or hairy, those sculptured thighs
    you'd die for, live for, no one
    showed you how to crave with your soul
    the forbidden joy between the legs,
    to long for same sex, man and boy.
    It came announced by nature with
    pubescent awakening, born between
    your legs and eyes, your red red mouth
    desiring young brother mouths.
    I remember still the young love laced
    with fear and gnarled with shame.

In the lockerroom naked men sashay
from shower to sauna with steaming skin,
undercover agents of lust.
Erections point like index fingers
at collective fantasies; wet dreams
ignite uncontrollable fires
fed by dumbbells and parallel bars
as muscles communicate like the thrust
of missiles whose launching pad is a crotch!

The gluteus maximus is more than
any man can stand! A raving madness
in the blood! I'm a casualty
of calipered curves, of lissome hips,
male mounds of maddening joy!
Beauty of buttocks! ecstasy of ass!
Those parts men love to gaze upon!
What butts! what balls! what divine cock!
I suffer anaphylactic shock
when I'm deprived of it.

Harold Norse
From *Gone With The Wind*

The first night in the boarding house
the landlady puts me in bed
with a fifteen-year-old kid. He thrashes
and flails, his legs all over mine,
hands grazing my belly. I scrunch
over to my side, thinking of jailbait
in Alabama, and shrivel up, aching
all night for him as he aches for me.
Next day I ask to change bedmates.
She puts me with the eighteen-year-old
whose hairy legs remained on his side
of the bed. Next night it's his brother,
the handsomest boy in Mobile. Southern
Baptists both. I was miserable.

In the room with the new blond kid
and the weightlifter, in separate cots,
at night I heard a flapping sound
starting and stopping. The full moon
rose over the weightlifter's cot
floodlighting his naked muscles,
white marble in moonlight, his hand
jerking, flapping, starting, stopping . . .
The blond kid snored and the weight-
lifter's physique glowed fantastically.
We all slept in the nude. Moonmad
in the heat, dripping with sweat, I crept
beside him, crouching, tense with desire,

and whispered his name, "Warren,
Warren!" He gave no sign of having
heard me. With the wild courage
of desperation I touched his thigh
and, startled, his body taut, he opened
his eyes and looked at me, then
at his rigid cock, and reached out gently,
fondling my hair, caressing my mouth....

Warren's asleep and Bud, the blond kid,
wakes and whispers, "C'mere!"
I can't believe my eyes. He's naked
and erect. He grabs my head
and I go down. Almost at once
he comes like a bull. Then:
"Don't *ever* do that again, hear!?"
"Didn't you like it?"
"We don't like cocksuckers in Alabama,"
he says smugly. "It's a crime against nature."
"It *is* nature!" I retort. "You *wanted* it!"
"Never mind! Jest stay in your bed, hear?
And leave Warren alone!" "That's Warren's business!"
"It's mine. If I catch you touching him
again, it'll cost you your job!"

At Dr. Terrell's on Royal Street
a fat young man painted
"lahk Picassio," had thinning,
fair flat hair, boozy blue eyes,
and an unpleasant habit of grabbing
my head and shoving it down
toward his crotch. I forced back his hands

each time and would have slugged him
but he was soft and would spatter.
He'd whip out his thin purple dick
and jerk off, hoping to elicit
some response. But a dog
would have been more tempting.
"Picassio" stopped talking only
when he masturbated. He drove
his old Ford through the streets shouting
obscenities at blacks when he drank.
Old Doc Terrell shuffled home
and sat in the library drinking,
exchanging a few words with
"Picassio" and glaring at me
as if it weren't World War Two,
and the Civil War hadn't ended,
and I was a spy in the house.

Harold Norse
Guatemalan Entry

I stare at the young hot cock throbbing
　　in tight white pants on my bed.
How long can I go on about travel fares and news of the day?
Dark smoldering eyes, half-sleepy, gaze at me
　　　　from a face the color of café au lait.

I'm anxious to strip this 19-year-old down again
and expose the rest of that dusk marble skin.
　　　　I stop talking and look at him.
He comes over and presses his huge hard-on
against my face and I turn my head
　　　　　　to kiss his pants there.

He begins to unbuckle his belt with the head of a bull
　　for a buckle and I smile and say *Toro*
　　　　and he smiles and says *Verdad*
and suddenly throbbing in the room in the sun
with chocolate skin darker than the rest of him
　　　　　　his cock appears.

He grabs my chest under the shirt
moving his strong hands down my thighs
　　white and hairy against his smooth darkness
　　and turns me around so that my back presses
　　　　　　against his cock
　　that he pushes between my buttocks
as he kneads my nipples in the sweltering heat
　　　　　of a lazy afternoon.

And we both begin to hump in a tropical trance
quickly reaching orgasm, he inside me,
I in my hand, as the madness boils over
and splashes onto my fist and drenches
the burning bed.

Scott O'Hara
Venice Beach: Memorial Day

Lying on the beach with Sir, tightly handcuffed
to the stakes he's driven at my hands and feet,
people strolling by, all unaware;
I can turn, rotisserate myself, but nothing more.
He relaxes, unconcerned, only attending me
to replace my beer each quarter-hour
—I suck them through a straw. 'Please Sir'—I say,
on finishing my third—'I need to piss…'
He looks at me, and at the crowded beach.
'Turn on your back,' he says, and I obey—
even bladder-bloated, hardon still won't go away,
tents my baggy running shorts—he smiles.
            'So piss,' he says.
The shorts are quickly soaked; the towel takes
a few more beers. Each time I ask—'Sir?' He nods,
and piss leaps up, bubbles through thin material,
puddles on my belly, as he watches.

Later, as I start to put the towel in the washer,
he corrects me. 'Save it.
      You can sleep with it tonight.'

Scott O'Hara
Spunk-boy

Spunk is what they call me
when they want me with a mohawk
when they want me up on stage
playing with The Criminal Classes
    …and they do, some of them
grovelling in the gutter, fawning on my feet
I can give them what they want—
they want a big dick & a foul mouth
a boot on the chest and one at the crotch
they want an old newspaper clipping,
not an 8x10 glossy
and I can dish it out in spades
I can be your Spunk, pig-boy
show you how I play my trade
just don't take me home at night
'cause then I might forget
instead of kicking you out of bed
making you sleep on the floor
    might cuddle up against you
        fall asleep and—accidental-like—
    kiss you on the eyes
When the eyes are closed, the cameras stop
the mirror fades, the lights are cut
even the director goes to sleep
and something changes
    Sure I'll be your spunk-boy, mister—
whaddya wanna pay?
    Ruffle up my mohawk and I'll curl
like a cat across your chest
    You want me for your Spunk-boy?

Scott O'Hara
Compton, CA:
Realidad y Fantasía

End of a work shift, they boarded the bus together:
2 Pancho Villa clones, 1 Latin Lover
    (flashing eyes, quick laugh, blue-black hair)
1 youth
—his age? impossible to even guess—
I'd have said, oh 22—with eyes that might be 50
a chin so soft it's never known the touch of razor
a quiet laugh, a frequent slow smile.
They chatted amiably—in Spanish—
a camaraderie of long acquaintance.
They may have been related.
The youngster's cowboy hat
    —straw, sun-faded—
pulled low, disguised his hair,
let his eyes shine softly out of shadow when he smiled.
When they got off the bus, one hour later,
not one of them lit a cigarette.

I followed after,
waylaid them at the entrance of an alley.
"I d like to suck you off. En grupo. I feel as though
you're everyone whose dick I've ever wanted…"
They took me, one by one,
into a warm and sheltered parking lot.
First uncles, in their fashion most excitable:
    two healthy servings of cock-cheese and sperm
    I'd swear they were identical twins:

equally appreciative.
Then father:
slow, methodical, becoming passionate
positively uncontrollable at orgasm.
He stayed to show his son the proper way to use a mouth
stood behind him stroked his arms, cupped his flexing butt
and kissed him as he came.

Scott O'Hara
"There is something of the comfort"

There is something of the comfort
of a steaming cup of cocoa
in taking cock in hand and gently
beating up a frothy bowl of cream.
In just a few more strokes
—as all the cookbooks caution you—
your knees will turn to butter.

Scott O'Hara
All in the Mind

I watched them playing, watched the interplay
I watched his butt grow cherry-red
his dick grow hard, start dripping
Joe's wrist grow tired—
    Here, you take over for awhile, he said—
and handed me the belt.
With fear and trembling I approach
a butt I've loved since I was young
a butt that keeps me feeling young
to stroke and kiss it makes my   Slash!
my arm on automatic pilot cuts through memory
Joe watches, rests, approves
    —his hardon tells me so
and mine respects the stimuli as well.
This is not what I expected when I called:
I called on Marc as one may visit childhood friends,
not sure if there is still a common thread
    —no threads, exactly, but the ropes
suspended from the ceiling, on his bed
said there was something to be shared
—I'd like for you to meet my Lover—
Apprehension: the innocence I knew, where is it?
    I'd like to meet him too.
And now I've driven him to sobs
a dick that's harder than I ever knew it
    —If I had known this years ago
might we be lovers still?—
Joe's knowing eyes go through me;

his fingers twist Marc's tits and trigger climax
    the butt uplifts for more, AAAH!
I hand him back the belt, respectfully, and suddenly
—I don't know how—I find myself down on my knees
worshipping his boots.

Scott O'Hara
On the Beach in Capri

I had a dick enrapt between my lips. A very blonde,
  Germanic dick,
and not at all Italian; but attractive, stiff, uncircumcised,
and relatively eager for release. I wish the man had been
as willing—but, with sand declining quickly in his extra-
  large
exceptional egg-timer balls, he suddenly recanted: pulled
his dick away, smiled at me as if to say, "Please, no
  offense"—
when I stood up, he gave my dick a squeeze, just out of
  curiosity—
and, repositioning his stone-like hard-on (obvious & leaden,
  there,
within his swimmers), he—the fool!—simply stepped into the
  water,
and was gone. I watched him swim away, as my erection
  slowly faded.
He was strong and sure, and swam extremely well. But I
  must wonder
what it was that made him leave. I pride myself on my
Eulalian abilities: can he have been dissatisfied? His dick
would disagree… Oh hell, admit it: I am wounded in my
  vanity.

Orlando Paris
Sailor

Shyly you undress
With your back to me,
Lifting your navy jumper
Over your tousled head,
Kicking off your shoes
And dropping your blue
Bell-bottoms in a heap,
And stand, legs apart,
In T-shirt and skivvies,
Just long enough to excite
Me even more, and then
You strip completely, as
I have done, and turn
To face my waiting arms,
My surging cock and
Tensed-up balls, watching
My eyes to see if I
Am shocked by your
Enormous erection totally
Tattooed as a black cobra,
It's tail encircling your balls
And hanging down your thigh.
I drop to my knees and—
How many times have you heard this?—
Beg you to spit venom down my throat.

Orlando Paris
Dear John

Thank you for all your letters,
Not because they are full of news
Of you, or because they tell me
Your innermost thoughts; as a matter of fact,
They are kind of dull, which is okay,
So I can leave them around
For my parents to read; but
Because of the pubic hairs you
Mailed to me, and because the drops of
Your sperm are like dried tears
On the paper for me to sniff, just
Faintly discerning the odor of
Your load, happy in the knowledge
That you were thinking of me
When you jerked off overseas.
Oh, by the way, did I tell you?
I met this other terrific guy in
School who's just dying to meet you
When you get out of the Navy.

Orlando Paris
My Hero

There, on the locker room floor,
Just as I have stripped nude,
I see his jock-strap lying, dropped
In a little heap, the narrow
Bands of webbed elastic flowing
Casually over the form-fitting pouch,
Bulging hugely, though empty,
Testimony to the great size of
The warm, soft burden it protects
In its damp, stained folds.
Trembling, I bend over and
Pick it up, handling it as I would
A precious jewel, a sacred thing,
And bring it to my nostrils and
Breathe deep, inhaling the perfume
Of his sweat, the aroma of his
Oft-dribbled urine, and the memory
Of some glorious concealed ejaculation
When our high school cheered.
I hold it to my lips and am
Tongue-kissing it when he returns
From the showers and smiles and,
Noticing how hard I am,
Proud of my love for him,
Tells me I can keep it if
I will let him wear mine.

Orlando Paris
Initiation

Pleasure is multiplied
In direct proportion
To the number of bodies,
I have learned after many
Solitary years of masturbation.
A few happier years of
Sixty-nine and being Lucky Pierre
Between two others, and now in
One glorious night, perfect
In harmony, soft light
And luxurious surroundings,
With perhaps a dozen
Mouths and tongues kissing,
Tickling, licking, sucking,
And rimming, and two dozen
Hands fondling, caressing, pinching,
Spanking, squeezing and scratching,
Two dozen balls to be licked,
And twelve aroused, slithering,
Inserting, ramming, shooting,
Slamming, dripping cocks
Getting hard again and again.
My senses are dulled and I begin
To wonder how many more
Drunken fraternity brothers
I can take before I pass out.

Orlando Paris
Phys. Ed.

In gym class I learned
The bicycle exercise: I lie
On my back, with my hands
Holding my hips high
Off the floor and
Pedal my feet in the air.
And now I await you
In the same position:
Ass high, held tight,
My ankles ready to lock
Behind your neck, pulling
Your face to mine, your
Lips to mine, your tongue
To mine while you slide in
And do push-ups.

Carl Phillips
The Hustler Speaks of Places
(after Langston Hughes)

I've known places:
I've known places weary as the flesh when it's had some,
    as rivers at last done with flowing.

My soul has been changed in places.

I mouthed a man dry in the Ritz-Carlton men's room.
I built a life upon a man's chest and, briefly, found peace.
I watched a man sleeping; I raised a prayer over his brow.
I heard the stinging, in bars, of lashes coming down on a
    man's bare ass, until it tore to the red that is sunset.

I've known places:
shaven, uncut places.

My soul has been changed in places.

Felice Picano
The Deformity Lover

The first one he loved—an accident
was a deaf mute
golden lean as a West Coast
basketball star.
Surprised by his luck
all he could think of was sex.
Until after
when they spoke on the sheets
writing messages in vaseline.
They met after that
once a week for some time.
The sex got hotter
their bodies fit better.
Then his speech began to slip.
Words seemed inexact
and harsh
compared to reading lips,
or making a point
with fingertip
or a kiss.
Then the deaf mute went away.

The next one was a blind boy
at a college gym dance.
A curly head of hair
the body of a stevedore,
an Adriatic address,
convinced him this would be special.

He wasn't disappointed.
This time they talked
but softly,
never looking at each other
in the bedroom's blinded night:
letting touches rediscover
soft steppes of ribs,
meadows of flesh,
seas of infinite skin.
They got together often—
geographers of the tactile.
Each visit left him thinking
our senses—
so misused when there—
when missing, are seldom missed.
Then the blind boy found a lover.

Since then he's gotten bolder
searching
for what others pass over.
An afternoon with a veteran
who happened to have left an arm
in a rice-paddy in Viet Nam
disproves that two hands
are better than one.
A night with someone older
whose seizures
when he's ready to come
aren't orgasm, but pre-*GRAND MAL*
becomes a game of sex
roulette.
Nothing indiscreet.

No ads in the paper for amputees.
No loitering near the handicapped
hoping a hunchback wants to connect.
It's beauty
not the grotesque he seeks.
But the only perfection he can see
is that most apparently,
poignantly
flawed.

This isn't a case from Kraft-Ebbing.
If asked,
he'd say he's a normal guy.
For him a chiseled profile is fine
but handsomer with a speech defect.
A well-defined chest will evoke
his desire
but heavily scarred or mispigmented
its athletic cut is more gratifying.
Deformity is a grace, he'll say.
Like courage, it's clean
and always naive,
open and free, no hiding—
the truest state of man perhaps.
Want to see him use this philosophy?
You can find him almost every night
in any one of a half dozen bars.
He's a hospital ward
for the maimed young gods:
a port for anyone's surgical storm:
looking to fuck
the human condition.

Mason Powell
Estoufee

I have you now,
Oh yes, I have you now,
All bound up, tied to the hard wood chair,
Your legs spread apart and leathered to the arms,
Your groin exposed.
Between your knees I build a dam,
A wooden board bound there,
Making your empty lap a triangle;
One wall wood,
Two walls thighs,
Your balls at the apex,
Tightening now with anticipation,
Above them your stiffening cock,
You have no idea what I will do.
You like that.
I have you now,
Oh yes, I have you now,
All bound up, tied to the hard wood chair.
I bring in the basket,
And you can hear the skittering,
The scraping inside.
Is that a drop of moisture at the end of your
     dick?
I open the basket and pour
Into the enclosure of your lap,
The many crawfish.
They wriggle, they wraggle,
Their tiny claws pinch and they try to escape,

Clawing their way up the sides,
Holding on with tiny pinchers.
You groan, you struggle,
Your cock spurts as I smile.
Later I cook the crawdads,
Cook up a spicy estoufee,
Season your nipped balls and dick
With Tabasco.
I pour the red dish down your chest,
Watch the sauce slide,
The little crustaceans tumble down your belly,
And then, while you stiffen,
While you thrash some more,
I eat it all out,
And you too.

Steven Riel
Arresting Sight

Every step he took was a sexual act,
a moving violation, a riotous
delight. The fuzz took notice.
Cabbies loitered at the light
to ogle him. Another guy, grey
& tweedy as Sherlock Holmes,
trailed him like a bloodhound.
Handcuffed, convicted—by desire—
I stalked him as well.
We were all accomplices
to this illegal demonstration,
this indecent exhibition.
His buns were so fresh,
they propositioned his shorts.
His centurion calves, Neanderthal thighs,
bulging billy club swung down the street.
There was no apprehending him.
He took it all in stride.

Eric Robertson
Clean Fun (in a Dirty World)

Some boys like hot cum, spattered on their faces,
      some like it on their stomachs and on their chests,
      some like its taste.
But my boy likes to dry fuck
      he loves the smell of hot air,
and when my lover dry fucks
      there ain't no fuck that can compare.

He knows just how to rub and play
      and throw his weight about my crotch,
and tease and grind through old blue jeans
      —his pelvic play is just too much.
I cum in a minute when he puts his strong tits
      tight up against my jeans' zipper
and baby, on the dance floor there's no one who sways
      oh quite the way he does—I'd lick him
all wet and dry, if only he'd let me—
      other boys love it, I know.
But my little lover gets all his jollies
      without ever taking off his clothes.

Eric Robertson
Gospel

"Oh, it's so big.
—Do you think it'll hurt?"
"Honey, it only hurts when it's small."

Eric Robertson
The Snodgrass of Heaven

There is a piggley, little wiggly
    that crawls right up a man's ass
giving him pleasure
all day, at his leisure
    without emotional harass.

A little dick, the size of a thick
    pickle, with a suppliant mind
that's easily trained
in pleasure and pain
    to squirm up a man's behind.

Its delicate crawl and wonderful drawl
    are heavenly lusts to indulge in;
its gingerly swirl
and leisurely curls
    are better than anything I've cum in.

Its wriggling fun, packed well in my buns
    gives me heaven that never tires;
wad after wad
that piggley cod
    fulfills my wildest desires.

Its orgasmic whorls, unfurl and unfurl
fulfilling my wildest desire.

Eric Robertson
Bad Sex

We lie here, open eyed
knowing something must be said
in the darkness; holding the sheets
like we're sleeping.

I should've asked if you like it
or gotten to know your rhythm
before we began to "fuck."

It takes a while,
sometimes too much;
you know, bad sex,
we ought to say something.

But the sheets are warm
and that's not why you came,
nor I, to feel discomfort.

Leigh W. Rutledge
Smart Boys Turn Me On

Forget men in leather
Or Armani sweaters,
Bartenders bore me
And drag queens just floor me,
Forget Mr. Benson
With his manly but dense grin—
Smart boys turn me on.

Thick glasses delight me
More than asses excite me.
Shorter or taller
What I want is a scholar;
Not a languid fellator
Or a grim masturbator,
But a boy who is handy
With a big calculator.
Oh, smart boys turn me on.

No, preppies don't do it,
And I always rue it
When I sleep with some bimbo
Whose wits are in limbo.
Now I save my erection
For boys of perception.
Yes, smart boys turn me on.

Not just average or bright,
And spare me the blight
Of intellectuals who think they're invincible.
What I want is an odd one
Who will give me a hard-on
Quoting Heisenberg's Uncertainty Principle.

So forget all those yuppies
(Or should I say guppies?)
Forget men of style
Flashing pierced tits and guile,
Forget Mr. Goodbar
And yesterday's porn star—
What makes them exciting
I haven't a clue.
My heart takes a jump,
And my cock goes straight up,
For a boy with a big fat I.Q.

Lawrence Schimel
On Men's Insecurities

What hangs between men's thighs
Has long confirmed their worth.
Men are measured by their size

And, without fail, they'll agonize,
Discontented with birth,
On what hangs between their thighs.

To compensate, each tries
To inflate his pecs' girth,
For men are measured by their size.

Still, it comes as no surprise,
When one's climbed into your berth,
What hangs between his thighs

Swells before your eyes,
Which betray gentle mirth.
Men are measured by their size

And now, when he dies
Le petit mort, no dearth
Hangs between his thighs
And you are measured by his sighs.

Lawrence Schimel
Abs Make the Heart Grow Fonder

What turns me on?
Sex-attraction is
so hard to define.

His parts must combine
to form a whole, I guess.
What really turns me on:

a tapering waistline
that underlines his
hard, well-defined

stomach. That's a sign
I can't resist because
it turns me on

like nothing else can,
really makes my penis
grow hard. To define

further wastes time;
if his stomach's
hard and defined
he'll turn me on.

John Dibelka writing as Jay Shaffer
Low Coups

LONG DISTANCE

If this was phone sex
how did these drops of your cum
land on my belly?

GENE E.

I dreamed of sucking
my own dick and woke to find
the dream mouth was yours.

CAVEMAN

His butt is like home
to me: so comfortable
I want to move in.

DICK SHUN NARY

Commitment defined:
An empty hole in my ass
only he can fill.

X

What do you do with
your ex-lover's lover? Smile?
Compare notes? Or fuck?

John Dibelka writing as Jay Shaffer
Number One

Vietnam
he said to answer
the one thing I never have asked him
except maybe
with my eyes.
I've never heard him cut off the country's name
the way the war cut off his body.
He cringes when his friends say
'Nam.

Sometimes
he cries at night.
Not so much
anymore.

The first time
I slept with him
he tried to strangle me.
When I got him woken up
he couldn't tell me
why.

So I held him
and I waited
for his tears and snot
to flush through the hair on his chest
and on mine
and mix with the jizz we had left there
in some former life

just the evening before
to make the mess that stuck us
     together.

     Guys
looked at us funny in bars
when we moved here they sneered
when I sat on the arms of his 'chair.
For his birthday I bought him a racer.
It's got no arms so now I sit
on the floor
at his feet
or where I figure
they'd be if they'd lived.

     We don't
go out much anymore
but we have lots of friends
to the house.
First time he answered
the door in his glory
I knew we'd get by.
I mean
what do you say
to a man with no legs
who greets you in a wheelchair
     naked?

     Just about
anything.
He's
     easy.

    My father
the Colonel
USMC (Retired)
wants to know
what we do in bed
but doesn't have the balls
    to ask.

    I laugh.
SIR!
Tough shit SIR!
No guts no glory.
No gory
    details.

    I don't know what
I'd tell the old man
even if he ever asked.
The truth
    I guess.

    I suck his dick
        Dad.
I fuck his ass
        face-up mostly
        sometimes face-down
        sometimes floating
        in the bathtub.
I ask him to suck me
            and fuck me
            and hold me
            and whisper to me in the dark

317

and he does.
I kiss him
and he kisses back.
I hold him when he needs it.
I carry him into the head when he's slept too late
and he has got to go
NOW.
And when he asks me
Why?
I always tell him
I don't know.

Or
maybe not.
Maybe the officer
doesn't deserve
the whole answer.
Maybe it's none
of his
business.

Maybe
to show my respect I would tell him
only of the things
that really
matter.

In our bed
I would say
the two of us just love each other.

And when I can see

on his face he is running
toward something
again in his dreams
I let him go
and watch him fly
and tell him
he's my hero.

John Dibelka writing as Jay Shaffer
For the Edification
of the Right Reverend
Young Mister Dodgson
—being a cautionary tale set in verse.

The light was shining right on me
    I posed with all my might
I did my very best to make
    my attitude a sight:
I scowled at every cruising man
    although I flagged to right.

The Master strode up forcefully
    took charge and told me, "Son,
you got no business to be here
    just teasing everyone.
It's downright rude," He growled, "but now
    we're gonna have some fun."

My sweat was wet as wet could be
    my mouth was cold and dry
I dared not ask for mercy for
    there was none in His eye;
no pleas were made for me by friends:
    I had no friends to cry.

This walrus-mustached carpenter
    gave me no chance to stand;
I tried to flee but He collared me
    with a swift and deadly hand:

I want a man, but not like this,
I thought; *my shit is canned.*

"And so to bed," I smiled and said
(my tongue was thick with fear)
"Or maybe just a handjob, and then,
afterwards, a beer?"
"I doubt it," spoke my Master, and
I almost shed a tear.

"I'm not too sure about all this,"
(my voice came out a screech)
"If we can talk now, while we walk
then maybe we can reach . . ."
He stuffed His handkerchief into
my mouth to end my speech.

My newfound Master looked at me
but not a word He said;
my newfound Master winked His eye
and shook His heavy head
to tell me that He did not choose
to take me to His bed.

For four long blocks we hustled up
the dark, deserted street;
my back was punched, my ass was kicked
my head hung in defeat:
And this was right, for now i knew
i'd end up at His feet.

At these blocks' end we turned and sped

down yet another four.
He pushed me fast. We came at last
up to a darkened door
He opened wide, shoved me inside
and threw me to the floor.

"Go strip your ass and clean it out.
Don't stop 'til I say so,"
He told me. Then He showed me
where He meant that i should go:
i did. Then, flushed and naked, stood
and waited, head hung low.

"The time has come," my Master said,
"to think of many things:
Of boots and whips and melting wax,
the lessons bondage brings,
and why a squealing slave is hot,
and hungry pigs in slings."

"But wait a sec," i tried to cry;
"Before we get to that.
Your new boy needs to catch his breath:
Your monster's way too fat."
"No rush," said He, backhanding me
a crack that sent me flat.

"An ass that's red," my Master said,
"is what we chiefly need.
A paddle, or My hand will do;
a nine-tailed cat, for speed:
you'll know I'm there; I'll warm you up,
not quite until you bleed."

You will like hell, i did not yell
　　although i wanted to—
i'd thought i'd wanted fucking, not
　　an ass all black and blue:
But deep inside, my need defined
　　exactly what i'd do.

The boy found out he soon would feel
　　what's good's not always nice;
i knew then that a kindness lurked
　　in every bare-assed slice:
This boy chose, then, to stand and bend
　　and learn to pay pride's price.

There was no shame—this was no game;
　　not just another trick:
i needed what i pleaded for
　　(although my sobs were thick).
My Master now said nothing, but
　　His paddle's swats came quick.

"I weep for you," He finally said;
　　"I deeply sympathize,"
as His belts strapped a new boy's yelps
　　and then subhuman cries.
At last, He held His handkerchief
　　before my streaming eyes.

"Oh baby," said my Master then;
　　"We've only just begun.
Now that you know that I'm in charge
　　and how this show is run

you can relax—enjoy the ride—
until we see the sun."

He laid me back. He stretched me out
He held me while i wept.
He told me all about Himself;
the company He kept.
He stroked my ass and when, at last,
He kissed my lips

i slept.

Aiden Shaw
"The neighbor's dog is a big fucker"

The neighbor's dog is a big fucker,
His tight black coat moves with his muscular body like a
    wet-suit.
I watch him.
He's inside and I'm outside.
He starts to get angry,
Pounding against the window, like he wants to mash me
    up, kill me.
I know he's alone in there,
So it's just him and me.

I get closer.
From here his face appears to be scarred across the cheek,
    mean, not ugly.
Now closer I can feel the pane as he thrashes against it.
Unbuttoning my jeans I pull them down over my swelling
    dick.
Taking a deep breath I squash up against the glass.
I feel the heat from his muscles.
He crashes powerfully,
I jump, excited, but return in seconds, glued to the
    window, to his strength.
Jesus,
He's gnawing at my dick,
He knows what it is.
He thrashes against my balls.
Each time it sends a deep thud through to my arse making
    me want to cum.

He scares the shit out of me,
Bringing me closer,
His huge shoulders,
Pounding me.
He'd kill me if he could.
So close,
He'd tear my balls off,
Squashed, hot against his face,
Shit,
He's looking right into my eyes,
He knows what's happening.
I shoot.
He starts to lick the window, my hot cum running down
over his face.
He can't hurt me.

Aiden Shaw
"I once kissed a boy who was dead"

I once kissed a boy who was dead.
His lips were tinged with purple.
His eyes showed no reaction.
I took off my clothes and lay down.
He was so cold that I felt cold beside him.
He gave me nothing which made me feel dead as well.
I fucked this boy.
Still he did not respond.
What is the point of this I thought.
Even if this is just for me,
Without response there is no joy.
When I thought I was finished he turned to me and said,
'My lips are tinted with purple,
They are bruised beyond belief.
I've been lying here such a long time that my skin is very
    cold.
My eyes have no reaction.
I do not want to hurt you,
Or see what could hurt me.
How can I give a response when all you did was fuck me.'

The Verb "To Adore"

To put the mouth to a handsome cock, down on my knees
    in something
like prayer, in the year of our Lord nineteen-hundred
    ninety-four,
in a semi-public place. He said he was nineteen, graced
    the light
brush of fluorescent lights with burnished balls, an
    ordinary boy wanting

to come. Another night stripped hurriedly to white briefs
    for which to be
grateful, and then to less than that, or more, the curl of
    pubic hair
and tensed thigh muscles, slight curvature in the thickness
of the aforementioned young cock. Now it's raining at five
    a.m.,

the last bus gone, the first not running yet, and I'm
    walking
the ten blocks home, alone and violently happy as a
    sudden
downpour easing into drizzle and a hint of hail, sharp
    taste

of early April in Chicago, fifty degrees. It takes courage to
    enjoy
unseasonable cold, dawn spilled across the as-yet-
    unstained sky
where Venus is a boy again, a pearl of semen or a morning
    star.

Reginald Shepherd
Nothing Looks the Same in the Light

Sucked him off at the End of the World
in Bennington, Vermont, where it was
cold, a tumble-down stone barrier
held off the shallow drop, held on
to moss and townie kids' graffiti,
damp grass and trampled dandelions
soaked through my denim knees, late
March, 1982, he said *I take a long time
to come*, then came, left, and the bitterness
surprised me when I expected salt,
so I forgot to spit it out, everyone
was sleeping or drinking or getting off
inside where lighted windows in dorms
said this is warm, this is locked doors,
walls and no moon, but better the dark
you know I thought, I swallowed and didn't
get off, got up, swallowed my doubts,
and in the morning we pretended
not to know each other, it wasn't big enough
for that, but room can be made,
there's always room to pretend by day.

Simon Sheppard
The Oral Tradition

I never cared too much for Jack Kerouac
till I saw a shot of him sprawled softly in a chair,
work boots untied, looking not like a legend
but like a man you'd want to fuck you
face down in some cheap hotel.
And I saw the particular flesh beneath his clothes,
touched the skin behind the name. Jack,
Jack Kerouac, let me worship at your feet,
lick your arch and instep. Please
shove your toes into my mouth
as you sit there with a hard-on
that's got nothing at all to do with
the art of the modern novel. Your
balls are in my hand, Jack,
I'm slapping them gently to make you moan.
I've got my tongue up your 1950s ass,
flicking it in and out, matting down the hairy corona.
Generations of lost adolescents
have worshiped your works, idolized you,
but it's *my* face in your ass, Jack,
gently working your asshole loose
as my mouth moves up to your ballsac.
Let me rub my lips in your wiry pubic hair;
I don't mind that you've murmured Neal's name.
Jack, I'm running my anxious tongue
up the underside of your cock.
You're shoving your famous dick down my throat
as I clutch my hands to your famous writer's ass.

I'm begging you, fill my mouth up with your jizz,
which'll taste salty-sweet just like anyone else's.
(Like Ginsberg said, humility is beatness.)
I'll grovel at your smelly feet
if you'll let me eat your cum.
What good is genius, good is fame,
what good is anything but this?
And when we're gone, we're real gone, man,
angels naked angels with angry broken hearts.
Desolation Angels
Desolation Angels
Desolation Angels
Jack
Jack
Jack
Beatnik

Simon Sheppard
The Perverts Seize Control
of the Means of Production

It's Labor Day and this is the
reward: the petit bourgeois beach,
families swimming with kids, just plain
normal folks screeching at each other,
building mortgaged sand castles, splashing

in the frigid tide. And out there,
not far from shore, in thigh-high
water, two fellows in their early 20s
wrestle, laughing, shiny
wet. One wiry, muscled, tan

in purple Speedos, the other paler,
chubby, not nearly so good-looking,
in baggy peach-colored trunks.
Around they go, reflecting sunlight like
a slap, grappling, twisting, clasped

front-to-back, belly to butt, dancing
out there in the surf. You wonder:
Those utilitarian, paunchy husbands,
broods at their sides, what are they
thinking? Do they notice the chubby one

as he glances down at his peach-colored groin,
where clinging fabric hides and reveals
his small, determined prick in earnest

erection? Does Purple Speedos notice?
How can he not? Just what do these two think
they're up to? (Been going on for far too long
to be a mere accident of cheerful male
aggression.) What'll happen next with these
guys, who slide against each other's naked
flesh, feigning a fight for supremacy? Do they

head for home, have a Bud, watch the baseball game?
Or will they gleefully draw the shades, slip cool
between starched sheets, and spill their
seed to no particular purpose? Well, it's comforting
that even here, amidst the grim imperatives

of "family vacation," the pleasure principle
insists on asserting itself. I can see it now:
Purple Speedos, grinning, pulls down Peach's
swollen trunks, hard dick springs upward forth,
Speedos buries his pretty face in blondish

pubic hair. Women scream, good fathers clap hands
over their sons' eyes. And some of us, a very
few, stand up on burning sand to cheer
this skirmish, this fleshy dialectic,
this salvo in the ongoing roar of battle,

this Glorious (September) Revolution.

(Just a wet dance, really.)

Simon Sheppard
The Burden of Selfhood

Slap me around he said please sir
so I know that I'm alive.
Take me to the edge of the world
where I won't know what I am.

Out in the rain we're out in the rain.
Get down on your knees I said.

Make it as painful as love he said
please make it as painful as love.

In the dark night
the night filled with cars.
You'll wear my leather collar
I said around your neck.

Yes sir he said oh yes yes sir.
And he looked up the rain
streaming down his vacant face.

(In his bed of cobras
the great god Vishnu sleeps,
afloat on the black lake of Infinity.
And what we call our world
is only Vishnu's dream.)

Get down on all fours
I said. And I slapped him

slapped him again and again
until dawn came up
and my hand and mind were numb.

Something had happened.
Nothing had happened.
I went home and slept the sleep
of the innocent. In whose fever dream?
In whose dark,
amazing dream?
Home and slept
the sleep of the gods
curled up against the dawn.

Simon Sheppard
A Shropshire Lad

As lewd as
green fucking nature is,
we met, hiking,
he was gleaming
coming toward me
on the trail.
Half my age
punked-out hair
loud Bermuda shorts
stiff nipples
spied through
an old Sex Pistols T-shirt.
Small talk
about the day,
then "I've gotta piss,"
I said, pulling it out,
arcing gold in his direction,
the purest essence of
poetry.
He was getting hard
inside his baggy shorts,
inside his teenage life.
"Now you
piss in your shorts,"
I said. He did,
piss running
hot down his leg.
I knelt to bathe

my face in it. We
dropped our packs,
I pulled his soggy
shorts off.
(If it
gives you a hard-on
it's done its job. If it
gives you
a hard-on,
it has.)
I took a handful
of the muck
I was kneeling in,
smeared it over
his smooth white thighs,
up the crack of his ass,
fingered it inside him
'til I felt hard shit
pushing back,
a sacrament of decay.
I had him down in the
mud now, legs up,
his hand pumping
away
on my cock.
And when later
we lay,
exhausted,
covered with piss and cum,
shit and mud and cum,
he looked up with dark,
hypothetical eyes

and said, "You
older guys,
all you think of
these days
is death."
I caught my breath and
told him about
the road kill
I'd seen that morning,
its unrecognizable,
stinking pelt
which someone had draped
on the interstate's
guard rail,
a neat but gaudy display.
And I stuck
my filthy hand
roughly
between his thighs
and felt him get hard
all over again. (His
beautiful secret prick.)
I never saw him again
after that.
But not a day goes by
I don't think of him.
High impact, big fate.
Not a day goes by.
Not yet…

Simon Sheppard
The Steep and Dangerous Path to Knowledge

This is the year
I started pissing on young guys,
golden liquid on the
bruised-red flesh of his ass,
the look in his eyes:
"I am facing my very own
abyss."

This is the month
when I carved out chunks
of stolen time.
We met behind his girlfriend's
back, we kissed,
he keeping his lips tight shut
until I forced in
my tongue,
made my spit flow
between us.

This is the day
I tore off his shirt, at last
pulled down his jeans,
him standing naked,
shivering nervous.
I slapped him across the cheek.
He whimpered, smiled,
said, "Thank you,
sir."

This is the hour
I fucked him as though
I were fucking Death.
With frenzy, disgust, and absolute
desire. To stifle his cries,
shoved my hand down his throat.
I slapped his ass,
my palm skidding on
hot sweat.

This is the minute
I knew I would love him always,
never could have him,
already had lost him forever.
I stroked his face
as one strokes an idiot child.
Dripping, he raised himself
from the filthy floor,
could barely stand himself
upright.

This is the instant
I ride into blinding light.
Where emptiness and lust collide,
I shoot a load of white-hot cum
down God's gaping throat.

This is the year
I dared to submit
to becoming
all that I really am...

David Trinidad
My Lover

My lover who is black
My lover who is blond
My lover who is Italian
My lover who is well-hung
My lover who sucks my toes
My lover who has thick lips
My lover who swallows my cum
My lover who licks my armpits
My lover who cums in my mouth
My lover who cums all over me
My lover who cums inside of me
My lover who has a perfect ass
My lover who wears a jockstrap
My lover who wears cowboy boots
My lover who pinches my nipples
My lover who likes Rachmaninoff
My lover who gives me gonorrhea
My lover who leaves his socks on
My lover who will not French kiss
My lover who doesn't know my name
My lover who fucks me standing up
My lover who sleeps on Vera sheets
My lover who is drenched with sweat
My lover who bleeds when I fuck him
My lover who completely undresses me
My lover who refuses to have safe sex
My lover who is my ex-lover's ex-lover
My lover who sucks my tongue when I cum

347

My lover who fucks me for the first time

My lover who plunges his tongue into my ear

My lover who drapes his legs over my shoulders

My lover who gropes me as I pass through the crowd

My lover who sticks three of his fingers up my ass

My lover who kisses me at midnight on New Year's Eve

My lover who rubs the crotch of his faded blue jeans

My lover who rapes me at knifepoint without lubricant

My lover who reaches into my pants while I play pinball

My lover who sucks me off in the bushes in Lafayette Park

My lover who presses his cock against mine as we slow
dance

My lover who licks a drop of pre-cum from the tip of my
dick

My lover who vomits on me in the middle of sex and passes
out

My lover who pulls me by the cock to a corner of the orgy
room

My lover who goes down on me in a parked car in the
pouring rain

My lover who pins my arms above my head and kisses me
long and hard

My lover who holds a bottle of amyl to his nose just before
he shoots his load

My lover who plays "Killing Me Softly With His Song"
over and over as we make love all afternoon

David Trinidad
The Boy

Looking back,
I think that he must have been an angel.
We never spoke,
but one entire summer, every day,
he sat on the curb across the street.
I watched him: thin, his skin white,
his blond hair cut short.
Sometimes, right after swimming,
his bathing suit wet and tight,
he would sit and dry off in the sun.
I couldn't stop staring.

Then late one night,
toward the end of the summer,
he appeared in my room.
Perhaps that's why
I've always considered him
an angel: silent, innocent, pale
even in the dark.
He undressed
and pulled back the sheet,
slid next to me.
His fingers felt for my lips.

But perhaps I am not remembering
correctly.
Perhaps he never came
into my room that night.

Perhaps he never existed
and I invented him.
Or perhaps it was me, not blond
but dark, who sat all summer
on that sunny corner: seventeen
and struggling to outlast
my own restlessness.

David Trinidad
At the Glass Onion, 1971

He stood behind me while I played pinball
in a corner of the bar. He rubbed his
hard-on against my jeans. It was the fall
after the rape. Nineteen, I was a wiz

at the game, but as he ran his large hand
along the inside of my thighs and said
how much he wanted to take me home and
fuck me, I glanced up at the flashing red

and white lights and let my last ball slide past
the flippers. Instead of getting more change,
as I'd said, I bypassed the bar and dashed
into the bathroom. No lock, though. "You're strange,"

he said, tugging. I looked down at his head
till someone knocked, stuffed my wet cock, and fled.

David Trinidad
Eighteen to Twenty-One

I

He said his name was Nick; later I learned
he'd crossed the country on stolen credit
cards—I found the receipts in the guest house
I rented for only three months. Over
a period of two weeks, he threatened
to tell my parents I was gay, blackmailed
me, tied me up, crawled through a window and
waited under my bed, and raped me at
knifepoint without lubricant. A neighbor
heard screams and called my parents, who arrived
with a loaded gun in my mother's purse.
But Nick was gone. I moved back home, began
therapy, and learned that the burning in
my rectum was gonorrhea, not nerves.

II

Our first date, Dick bought me dinner and played
"Moon River" (at my request) on his grand
piano. Soon after that, he moved to
San Diego, but drove up every week-
end to see me. We'd sleep at his "uncle"'s
quaint cottage in Benedict Canyon—part
of Jean Harlow's old estate. One night, Dick
spit out my cum in the bathroom sink; I
didn't ask why. The next morning, over

steak and eggs at Dupar's, Dick asked me to
think about San Diego, said he'd put
me through school. I liked him because he looked
like Sonny Bono, but sipped my coffee
and glanced away. Still, Dick picked up the bill.

III

More than anything, I wanted Charlie
to notice me. I spent one summer in
and around his swimming pool, talking to
his roommates, Rudy and Ned. All three of
them were from New York; I loved their stories
about the bars and baths, Fire Island, docks
after dark. I watched for Charlie, played board
games with Rudy and Ned, crashed on the couch.
Occasionally, Charlie came home with-
out a trick and I slipped into his bed
and slept next to him. Once, he rolled over
and kissed me—bourbon on his breath—and we
had sex at last. I was disappointed,
though: his dick was so small it didn't hurt.

IV

I made a list in my blue notebook: *Nick,
Dick, Charlie, Kevin, Howard, Tom...* Kevin
had been the boyfriend of an overweight
girl I knew in high school. I spotted him
at a birthday bash—on a yacht—for an
eccentric blonde "starlet" who called herself
Countess Kerushka. Kevin and I left

together, ended up thrashing around
on his waterbed while his mother, who'd
just had a breakdown, slept in the next room.
Howard was Kevin's best friend. We went for
a drive one night, ended up parking. His
lips felt like sandpaper, and I couldn't
cum—but I added his name to the list.

V

Tom used spit for lubricant and fucked me
on the floor of his Volkswagen van while
his ex-lover (also named Tom) drove and
watched (I was sure) in the rearview mirror.
Another of his exes, Geraldo,
once cornered me in Tom's bathroom, kissed me
and asked: "What does he see in you?" At a
gay students' potluck, I refilled my wine
glass and watched Tom flirt with several other
men in the room. Outside, I paced, chain-smoked,
kicked a dent in his van and, when he came
looking for me, slugged him as hard as I
could. It was the end of the affair, but
only the beginning of my drinking.

VI

I ordered another wine cooler and
stared at his tight white pants—the outline of
his cock hung halfway down his thigh. After
a few more drinks, I asked him to dance to
"The First Time Ever I Saw Your Face." He

pressed himself against me and wrapped his arms
around my neck. I followed him to his
apartment but, once in bed, lost interest.
I told him I was hung up on someone.
As I got dressed, he said: "If you love him,
you should go to him." Instead, I drove back
to the bar, drank more, and picked up a blond
bodybuilder who, once we were in bed,
whispered "Give me your tongue"—which turned me off.

VII

As one young guy screwed another young guy
on the screen, the man sitting a couple
seats to my right—who'd been staring at me
for the longest time—slid over. He stared
a little longer, then leaned against me
and held a bottle of poppers to my
nose. When it wore off, he was rubbing my
crotch. Slowly, he unzipped my pants, pulled back
my underwear, lowered his head, licked some
pre-cum from the tip of my dick, and then
went down on it. As he sucked, he held the
bottle up. I took it, twisted the cap
off and sniffed, then looked up at the two guys
on the screen, then up at the black ceiling.

Jonathan Wald
What's So Sexy About Synagogue?

I can only wonder
at what divinity inspired me
to masturbate under the table
as the Jews fled out of Egypt.

I'd like to say I had a vision
a rapturous glimpse of God
or at least some sexy, sandalled Egyptian
calling me to service from amidst the crowd—
it would have been less lonely.

I had found the bread of affliction
when athletic Andrew Allen showed me
my first pornography, straight—
"You have to admit, it tastes great!"—
my dick stiffened
as I bargained
flush and triumphant
I weighed a moment's gilded pleasure
against terror of my own desire
and then saw Andrew's ass—angelic
he bent over to kiss a fallen prayerbook
and the cup untasted

would not have been enough for me
rising briefly from degradation to dignity.
Instruction in friction was not on the syllabus;

I was self-taught, who was unable to ask,
by my sticky, awkward gait to the bathroom and
the permanent stains of shame and fear.

What shall you tell your child, on that day—
the duty of freedom to free someone else—
to celebrate his people? Of two boys,
survivors of plagues buoyed by flight
sneaking a kiss under sheltering palms,
rearranging tunics and teffilin, then
scrambling to rejoin their exodus in time
to escape the watery wrath of God.

Theirs is the history I study *sub rosa*,
under the table, in solitary glory
unaided by portents or other messengers—
not one of miracles but of their aftermaths
the Jews in the desert for fifty years
in the time of bondage the hope of redemption
creeping through terror towards ecstasy.

Jonathan Wald
What's So Sexy About Speedos?

Just say the word
lighting briefly on the ee's
hurrying through to
the surprise ending,
to the final Oh!
the possibilities,
just barely contained,
a Rorschach test
of sexuality.

Then say it lovingly.
Let your lips linger
like that, at the end,
reaching, pursed, ready.
Free associate:

pouch pool pull press.
Scientists will discuss
streamlining, resistance, hydro-
dynamics. Don't be
distracted. Ask them:
Is there a measurement
for ease of removal?

There is magic in spandex and elastic
that no physics can explain.

If it helps, picture them at
design meetings, examining
new innovations in contour
with a growing excitement
which they pull their lab coats
across their laps to hide.

This is fun! Picture swimsuit
models picturing nuns,
window dressers turning
backs to ogling crowds,
department store sales clerks
taking three deep breaths
in the dressing rooms,

and next time you're at the pool,
and you see a man,
suited, sexy, poised
to dive, or dripping,
looking somewhere
else, breathe a silent sigh
of thanks, your eyes
all drawstrings and logos
to the scientists, hands
tense in pristine pockets,
always reminding you
your imagination
is your greatest lover.

L. E. Wilson
Ho-Ho-Ho

I think that Santa must've been a hunk
at thirty-five or forty, when the pounds
were just beginning to expand his saint-
ly waist, when hair and beard were lightly touched
with silver frost, and little boys (like me
who sat upon his lap might get their wish.

Forget the toybag full of store-bought junk!
I much prefer the manly belly round
with hedonistic living, and a faint
distinctive smell of male musk. I'm such
a sucker for a bearded smile, see
for burly, hairy guys who don't, well, swish.

Give me the man inside the velvet red,
I'll entertain him well in winter's bed.

L. E. Wilson
On Trains

strangers
on trains
in jeans
grey flannel
black leather
and denim
old and young
it's only
the men
who catch my eye
behind
every zipper
is a cock
which might
or might not
thrill
to the touch
of a tentative hand
better
a handsome man
better
tall and blond
ruddy
and rich
but
behind
every zipper
is a cock

which might
or might not
now
tremble
at the lick
of a shy tongue

Gregory Woods
"Enough of this chatter"

Enough of this chatter.
Leave your political
opinions and vague

aspirations behind.
Come to bed. I want
to know how you taste

but not your tastes,
how you feel but not
what pass for feelings.

I crave nothing but
to hold forth with your
articulate flesh.

Gregory Woods
"A goatboy pissing"

A goatboy pissing
between roots, sweet vapour
of urine and pine,

turns to me grinning,
still pissing, barefoot
in heat of wet needles,

back to his careless herd.
By way of introduction
we gossip soccer

and he goes on and on
naming English teams
as I go down on him.

Gregory Woods
"I purloined the pleasures"

I purloined the pleasures
greedy children find
in mere honeypots,

light-fingered between
the pale haunches of
an eighteen-year-old.

Flaunting his lavish
glamour, he scattered
unforeseen largesse

of silver, his hole
convulsed like the drawstrings
of a spendthrift's purse.

Gregory Woods
"The straitlaced fister"

The straitlaced fister
takes a puppet-master's
view, putting you on

like new opera gloves,
attentive to his nails
lest he ladder you.

Hoodwinked by his own
vanity, he consults
you like a wrist-watch

as if expecting
something to happen
that isn't going to.

Gregory Woods
The Coelacanth

I knelt to press my face
Into the muscles of his arse
As a penitent will nestle
In the pages of his missal.

Has any tongue been thrilled
At such inconsequential length
Since Adam for sheer pleasure called
The coelacanth the coelacanth?

Gregory Woods
Hereafter

The dead porn boy is still
doing it, coming time
and again as if taken
    by surprise,

no better prepared than
the innocent he looks
for this convulsion of
    old pleasures.

From his raucous breath and
the sticky glamour of
his belly, we who watch
    him glean our

unlikely luck, compelled to
remember him each time,
oblivious, he wets our
    handkerchiefs.

In time his repertoire
of masks will seem rehearsed.
refined, impulsive as
    kabuki,

and we'll have taught ourselves
to duplicate his gestures
out of deference to the
    tradition.

But unlike the Jesus
weltering in sweat on
a gold chain across his
    collar bone,

we won't get any nearer
godliness than when he
spreads his legs and lifts his
    shaggy arse.

Gregory Woods
My Lover Loves

My lover loves me with kid gloves.
That is, no matter who's above
    And who beneath
    We use a sheath—
We never screw without a Condom.

He holds me in such high regard
He shields me like a bodyguard.
    Although love's dart
    Has hit my heart,
He fired it safely in a Condom.

Whenever he comes home from work
He brings me bribes, inducements, perks;
    But of his gifts
    The one that lifts
My spirit most's a pack of Condoms.

Although his clothes are always fine
(Comme des Garçons and Calvin Klein)
    He looks his best
    When he's undressed—
Yet even better in a Condom.

As long as he takes care of me
I am not scared of HIV.
    My lover loves
    Me with kid gloves
But loves me most of all with Condoms.

Ian Young
Home on the Range

"Oh! Cisco!"—Leo Carillo
"Oh! Pancho!"—Duncan Renaldo

Have you ever thought about how
those handsome young heroes in the western movies
so often have sidekicks to help them,
inseparable older companions, familiar yet
oddly deferential,
always taking the lead from the younger guy?
A curious relationship when, you think of it
What keeps the older man riding just a little behind
his lean young friend?
And why does our hero keep him around?
Sometimes the sidekick is stout and cantankerous
(in which case he would be played by Edgar Buchanan)
and sometimes long in the tooth and funny (Gabby Hayes).
Or he might be wise, stoical and a little sad (Ben Johnson).
Best of all, when the young traveller has no name
and looks like Clint Eastwood,
his older friend is quiet, tough and hot
and is Lee Van Cleef.
Once or twice Lee has saved Clint's life in a tight spot.
Even so, Lee figures he still owes Clint.
Owes him a lot.
So gunman and sidekick ride together and
face down the opposition (they're always outnumbered):
the sheriff and his posse, the bad guys, or the town.
Then they ride out when the job's done and

make camp for the night
cooking beans and bacon over an open fire,
crickets and the occasional wolf supplying the music.
They don't say much to each other, just a word or
two now and then, spitting into the fire.

Why do they ride together then, these two?
What strange hold does the young gunman have over his
    friend?
Does it ever occur to you
we never see these guys at home. Do they have a home?
Actually they do:
a comfortable ranch-house
with some ground around it for cattle,
dogs and now and then a young trail-hand or two
brought in to help with the chores and provide some
company.
So let's look in on them.
We'll say it's Clint and Lee this time,
just to be sexy about it.
Lee's a dangerous man but Clint
knows how to handle him and
has Lee haul in more wood while
Clint lounges in the big chair in front of the log fire,
one leg slung over the chair arm. He's
cleaning his gun and
watching his friend sweat.
He's half asleep but keen as a coyote,
a little smile playing on his lips.
He snaps his fingers and Lee
drops to his knees and
nuzzles Clint's swelling blue-jeaned crotch.

Clint takes his time rolling a cigarette.
Lee lights it, striking the match with one hand.
Clint offers him the first puff. The test is Clint's as
Lee, on his knees, has other things to do with his face.
Clint's strong hand ruffles the balding head between his
    legs
and a brass fly-button
pops out of its slit.
He takes off his belt, runs it
through his hands like a fresh-shot rattler and
cracks it, suddenly, like a lariat.
Lee hisses and feels Clint's boot on his neck. It creaks.
The fire is hot on his back and rear. The saddle
lying on the buffalo rug
shines in the orange flame-light.
It'll be a long, cold night outside,
but warm in here, for them.
"I want it, boss," Lee whispers.
The tobacco-stained hand, one finger-joint missing,
gently strokes the young gunman's thigh.
"Earn it then."
(His eyes narrow to slits; his teeth clench.)
"Earn your pay." (The pay packet
seems to be growing as Lee fondles it,
thinking about a bonus.)

In the bunkhouse, the new hired hands,
real goodlooking, both of them, but just boys,
have stripped to their longjohns and are fooling around
tying each other up with rawhide by the light of an oil lamp,
thinking about Clint and Lee.

CONTRIBUTORS

Antler, a well known eco-poet and activist, is the author of *Factory* (City Lights) and *Last Words* (Ballantine) and has appeared in innumerable journals and anthologies. He is the winner of the Walt Whitman Award and the Witter Bynner Prize from the American Academy and the Institute of Arts & Letters, among other awards, and he lives in Milwaukee with Jeff Poniewaz.

Robin Wayne Bailey is the author of numerous fantasy novels, including the "Brothers of the Dragon" series (Roc Books) and the forthcoming *Shadowdance* (White Wolf). He lives in Kansas City.

David Bergman is the author of two books of poetry, *Cracking the Code*, winner of the George Elliston Poetry Prize, and *The Care and Treatment of Pain*, and is the editor of many books, including: *The Violet Quill Reader* and the "Men on Men" series. He lives in Baltimore.

Dick Bettis lives in Brooklyn. He has published fiction in *Christopher Street*, and has just completed a novel, *Guy*.

Mark Bibbins has published poems in *The Paris Review*, *The Olivetree Review* and other publications. He lives in Manhattan.

Walta Borawski was the author of two volumes of poetry, *Sexually Dangerous Poet* (Good Gay Poets Press) and *Lingering in a Silk Shirt* (Fag Rag Books).

William Bory was the author of one volume of poetry, *Orpheus in His Underwear* (Cythoera Press). He lived in Manhattan.

Jonxavier Bradshaw lives in San Francisco.

Eric Brandt is a publicist for HarperSanFrancisco, and has published in *Christopher Street*. He lives in San Francisco.

Perry Brass is the author of numerous books, all published by Bellhue Press: *Sex Charge* (poetry), *Mirage* (novel), *Works* (stories), *Out There* (stories), and his most recent, *Albert, Or the Book of Man* (novel). He lives in New York City.

James Broughton is the author of numerous books of poems, including *Ecstasies, Graffiti for the Johns of Heaven, Hymns to Hermes, Songs of the Godbody, The View from the Top of the Mountain*, and others. He lives in Washington State.

Regie Cabico is a performance artist who's appeared on MTV and a poet whose work has appeared in various anthologies and periodicals. He lives in Manhattan.

Rafael Campo's first book of poems, *The Other Man Was Me* (Arte Publico) won the National Poetry Series, and a second book, *What the Body Told*, is due from Duke University. He is also the author of a book of essays, *The Poetry of Healing: A Doctor's Education in Empathy, Identity, and Desire* (W. W. Norton).

Marsh Cassady is the author of thirty-nine books in a variety of genres and media, including novels, plays, and textbooks. He lives in Southern California.

Steven Cordova works for the Gay Men's Health Crisis and is writing a sequence of poems about the Lower East Side of Manhattan, where he lives. This is his first sale.

Alfred Corn is the author of numerous volumes of poetry, including *The Western Door* and *Children of Paradise*. He lives in Manhattan and teaches at Columbia University.

Peter Daniels is the author of two volumes of poetry, *Peacock Luggage* and *Be Prepared*, and editor of two anthologies from Oscars Press, *Take Any Train: Gay Men's Poetry* and *Jugular Defenses: An Aids Anthology*. He lives in London.

Gavin Geoffrey Dillard is the author of numerous books of poetry, including: *Yellow Snow*, *The Naked Poet*, and *Pagan Love Songs*. He lives in Southern California.

Mark Doty won the National Book Critics Circle Prize for his volume of poetry, *My Alexandria*. His most recent book is *Atlantis* (HarperCollins). He lives in Province-town.

David Eberly is the author of a book of poetry, *What Has Been Lost* (Good Gay Poets), and has just completed a second volume, *Last Call*. He lives in Boston.

Edward Field's collected poems, *Counting Myself Lucky*, was published by Black Sparrow Press. He lives in Manhattan.

Allen Ginsberg won widespread fame for his book *Howl* (City Lights Press). His *Collected Poems* was just published by HarperCollins, along with a new volume, *Cosmopolitan Greetings*. He lives in Manhattan.

Thom Gunn's *Collected Poems* were recently published by Farrar Strauss & Giroux. He is the author of eleven previous collections, including: *The Man With Night Sweats, My Sad Captains, Moly, The Passages of Joy, Jack Straw's Castle*, and others. Born in England, he's made his home in San Francisco since 1954.

Peter Hale lives in New York, where he works for Allen Ginsberg.

Trebor Healey is the author of three chapbooks of poetry: *Emotional Hardware, The Queer Love of Comrades*, and *Whitecloud Eating Rain*, and co-editor of *Beyond Definition* (Manic D Press), a collection of fiction and poetry by gay and lesbians writers living in San Francisco.

Scott Hightower has published poetry in *The Paris Review, Salmagundi, Bay Windows*, and numerous other journals. He lives in Manhattan, teaches at Fordham University, and also leads a poetry workshop at the Gay Men's Health Crisis.

Richard Howard is the author of ten volumes of poetry, and has translated over a hundred books from the French. He won the Pulitzer Prize in 1971 for *Untitled Subjects*, and the American Book Award for his translation of Baudelaire's *Les Fleurs du Mal*. He is Poet Laureate of New York State, and poetry editor of *The Paris Review*. He divides his time between Manhattan and Houston.

Abraham Katzman is a new poet whose work has appeared in *Exquisite Corpse, Frighten the Horses, Diseased Pariah News,* and the anthology *Badboys, Barbarians, and Gents* (Alyson). He lives in Seattle.

Dennis Kelly is the author of two collections of poetry, *Chicken* and *Size Queen* (both published by Gay Sunshine). He lives in Seattle.

Rudy Kikel is the author of *Lasting Relations* and *Long Division*. He is an editor at the newspaper *Bay Windows*, and edited the anthology of new gay poets *Badboys, Barbarians and Gents* for Alyson Publications.He lives in the Boston area.

Victor King, whose work appears regularly in *Drummer, Mach,* and similar magazines, and in John Preston's *Flesh and the Word* anthologies, lives in Manhattan.

Wayne Koestenbaum is the author of two volumes of poetry, *Ode to Anna Moffo* and *Rhapsodies of a Repeat Offender*; a book of literary criticism, *Double Talks: The*

Erotics of Male Literary Collaboration; and two non-fiction
books, *The Queen's Throat: Opera Homo-sexuality and
Desire* (a National Book Award nominee) and *Jackie Under
My Skin*. He teaches at Yale University.

Michael Lassell won the Lambda Literary Award for his
volume of poems *Decade Dance* (Alyson). He is the author
of one other collection of poetry, *Poems for Lost and Un-
Lost Boys* (Amelia), and a book of prose and poetry, *The
Hard Way* (Richard Kasak). He edited *The Name of Love:
Classic Gay Love Poems*, for St. Martin's Press. He lives in
Manhattan.

David Laurents is the editor of two other Badboy
anthologies, *Wanderlust: Homoerotic Tales of Travel* and
Southern Comfort. His stories and poems have appeared in
Honcho Overload, First Hand, Steam, Stallions and Other
Studs (PDA Press) and other anthologies and magazines.
He lives in Manhattan.

Timothy Liu is the author of two collections of poetry,
most recently *Burnt Offerings* (Copper Canyon Press). He
lives in Iowa.

Michael Lowenthal is the editor of The Best of the
Badboys and T*he Badboy Erotic Library* vols. I and II,
and co-editor with John Preston of *Flesh and the Word 3*
and *Friends and Lovers*. He lives in the Boston area,
where he writes regularly for *The Boston Phoenix* and
many gay and lesbian newspapers across the country.

John McFarland lives in Seattle.

Rondo Mieczkowski lives in Los Angeles and has published fiction and poetry in various journals and anthologies, including *Diseased Pariah News* and *Blood Whispers 2: L.A. Writers on AIDS*.

Edmund Miller is the author of a book of poetry, *Fucking Animals* (STARbooks), and a chapbook, *The Happiness Cure*. He is the chairman of the English Department of C.W. Post University.

M. S. Montgomery is the author of a book of sonnets, *Telling the Beads*. He is a librarian at Princeton University.

Carl Morse, a poet and playwright, is the author of a book of poems, *The Curse of the Future Fairy*, and co-editor of the seminal volume, *Gay and Lesbian Poetry in our Time* (St. Martin's Press). He lives in Manhattan and is director of publications at the Museum of Modern Art.

Christopher Murray founded and runs, Vox Positiva, a writing workshop for people living with HIV funded by Broadway Cares/Equity Fights AIDS and administered by the Actors Fund of America. He lives in New York City.

Harold Norse is the author of twelve books of poetry, including: *Hotel Nirvana* (City Lights), *Carnivorous Saint* (Gay Sunshine), and *The Love Poems* (Crossing Press). He has also written an autobiography, *Memoirs of a Bastard Angel*. He lives in San Francisco.

Scott O'Hara, an ex-porn actor who used to be known as "the biggest dick in San Francisco," is the publisher and editor of *Steam* Magazine and PDA Press, which has recently begun a new magazine, *Wilde*. He lives in Wisconsin and San Francisco.

Orlando Paris was the pseudonym for author Paul O. Welles, and author of numerous volumes from Greenleaf Classics, including *The Short Happy Sex Life of Stud Sorrell and 69 Other Flights of Fancy*, from which these poems are drawn.

Carl Phillips won the Morse Prize in Poetry for *In the Blood* (Northeastern University) and a second volume of poetry, *Cortege*, from which this poem is drawn, is forthcoming from Graywolf. He is teaching at Harvard this year.

Felice Picano, a member of the Violet Quill, is the author of many books, including: *The Joy of Gay Sex* (HarperCollins), *Ambidextrous* (Hard Candy), *Men Who Loved Me* (Hard Candy), *Like People From History* (Viking), *The Lure, Eyes, The Deformity Lover* (Gay Presses of New York), etc. He lives in Manhattan and is a member of the Publishing Triangle.

Mason Powell lives in the San Francisco Bay Area where he edits for *Manifest Reader* and contributes to a number of leather and skin magazines.

Steven Riel is the author of a book of poems, *How to Dream*, and the poetry editor of *RFD: A Country Journal for Gay Men Everywhere*. He lives in Massa-chusetts and works as a librarian at Harvard University.

Eric Robertson works on Wall Street by day and is a poet by night.

Leigh W. Rutledge is the author of numerous books, including *Gay Decades*, *The Gay Book of Lists*, *Dear Tabby*, *The Lefthander's Guide to Life*, *It Seemed Like a Good Idea at the Time*, and others. He lives in Florida.

Lawrence Schimel's poetry and fiction has appeared in over sixty anthologies, including *The Random House Treasury of Light Verse*, *Dark Angels: Lesbian Vampire Stories*, and *Weird Tales from Shakespeare*, and in numerous periodicals, including: *The Tampa Tribune*, *The Saturday Evening Post*, *Physics Today*, *The Writer*, etc. He lives in Manhattan.

John Dibelka writing as Jay Shaffer is the author of a handful of books of gay erotica, including *Animal Handlers* and *Full Service*; and he has appeared in the anthology *Doing it for Daddy*, edited by Pat Califia (Alyson).

Aiden Shaw is a well-known (and well-hung) porn actor. He has written a novel, *Brutal*, and is working on a new novel.

Reginald Shepherd is the author of one volume of poetry, *Some are Drowning* (Pittsburgh). He holds an M.F.A. from the University of Iowa and currently lives in Chicago.

Simon Sheppard's poetry has appeared in *The James White Review, Art & Understanding, Five Fingers Review, Black Sheets*, and *Inciting Desire*, as well as in the anthologies *Beyond Definition* and *A Loving Testimony*. He lives in San Francisco.

David Trinidad is the author of five books of poetry, including *Answer Song* (High Rick), *Hand Over Heart: Poems 1981–1988* (Amethyst), *Pavane, November*, and *Monday, Monday*. He lives in New York City.

Jonathan Wald now lives in San Francisco. These are his first poetry sales.

L.E. Wilson has appeared in the anthology *Badboys, Barbarians, and Gents* (Alyson Press) and in various journals. He lives in the Midwest.

Gregory Woods is the author of one book of poems, *We Have the Melon* (Carcanet) and two non-fiction books, *Articulate Flesh: Male Homo-Eroticism in Modern Poetry* (Yale University) and *This Is No Book: A Gay Reader* (Mushroom Publications). He teaches at Nottingham Trent University, England.

Ian Young edited the first-ever gay male poetry anthology, *The Male Muse*, and its sequel, *Son of the Male Muse*. He writes a regular book review column for *Torso* and contributes poems to many magazines and journals. He splits his time between Ontario and British Columbia.

The Masquerade Erotic Newsletter

Free GIFT

BADBOY

JOHN PRESTON

Tales from the Dark Lord II $4.95/176-4

The second volume of acclaimed eroticist John Preston's masterful short stories. Also includes an interview with the author, and an explicit screenplay written for pornstar Scott O'Hara. An explosive collection from one of erotic publishing's most fertile imaginations.

Tales from the Dark Lord $5.95/323-6

A new collection of twelve stunning works from the man *Lambda Book Report* called "the Dark Lord of gay erotica." The relentless ritual of lust and surrender is explored in all its manifestations in this heart-stopping triumph of authority and vision from the Dark Lord!

The Arena $4.95/3083-0

There is a place on the edge of fantasy where every desire is indulged with abandon. Men go there to unleash beasts, to let demons roam free, to abolish all limits. At the center of each tale are the men who serve there, who offer themselves for the consummation of any passion, whose own bottomless urges compel their endless subservience.

The Heir•The King $4.95/3048-2

The ground-breaking novel *The Heir*, written in the lyric voice of the ancient myths, tells the story of a world where slaves and masters create a new sexual society. This edition also includes a completely original work, *The King*, the story of a soldier who discovers his monarch's most secret desires. Available only from Badboy.

Mr. Benson $4.95/3041-5

A classic erotic novel from a time when there was no limit to what a man could dream of doing.... Jamie is an aimless young man lucky enough to encounter Mr. Benson. He is soon led down the path of erotic enlightenment, learning to accept cruelty as love, anguish as affection, and this man as his master. From an opulent penthouse to the infamous Mineshaft, Jamie's incredible adventures never fail to excite—especially when the going gets rough! First serialized in *Drummer*, *Mr. Benson* became an immediate classic that inspired many imitators. Preston's knockout novel returns to claim the territory it mapped out years ago. The first runaway success in gay SM literature, *Mr. Benson* is sure to inspire further generations.

THE MISSION OF ALEX KANE

Sweet Dreams $4.95/3062-8

It's the triumphant return of gay action hero Alex Kane! This classic series has been revised and updated especially for Badboy, and includes loads of raw action. In *Sweet Dreams*, Alex travels to Boston where he takes on a street gang that stalks gay teenagers. Mighty Alex Kane wreaks a fierce and terrible vengeance on those who prey on gay people everywhere!

Golden Years $4.95/3069-5

When evil threatens the plans of a group of older gay men, Kane's got the muscle to take it head on. Along the way, he wins the support—and very specialized attentions—of a cowboy plucked right out of the Old West. But Kane and the Cowboy have a surprise waiting for them....

Deadly Lies $4.95/3076-8

Politics is a dirty business and the dirt becomes deadly when a political smear campaign targets gay men. Who better to clean things up than Alex Kane! Alex comes to protect the dreams, and lives, of gay men imperiled by lies.

Stolen Moments $4.95/3098-9

Houston's evolving gay community is victimized by a malicious newspaper editor who is more than willing to sacrifice gays on the altar of circulation. He never counted on Alex Kane, fearless defender of gay dreams and desires everywhere.

Secret Danger $4.95/111-X

Homophobia: a pernicious social ill hardly confined by America's borders. Alex Kane and the faithful Danny are called to a small European country, where a group of gay tourists is being held hostage by ruthless terrorists. Luckily, the Mission of Alex Kane stands as firm foreign policy.

Lethal Silence $4.95/125-X

The Mission of Alex Kane thunders to a conclusion. Chicago becomes the scene of the right-wing's most noxious plan—facilitated by unholy political alliances. Alex and Danny head to the Windy City to take up battle with the mercenaries who would squash gay men underfoot.

JAY SHAFFER

Shooters $5.95/284-1

A new set of stories from the author of the best-selling erotic collections *Wet Dreams, Full Service* and *Animal Handlers*. No mere catalog of random acts, *Shooters* tells the stories of a variety of stunning men and the ways they connect in sexual and non-sexual ways. A virtuoso storyteller, Shaffer always gets his man.

Animal Handlers $4.95/264-7

Another volume from a master of scorching fiction. In Shaffer's world, each and every man finally succumbs to the animal urges deep inside. And if there's any creature that promises a wild time, it's a beast who's been caged for far too long.

Full Service $4.95/150-0

A baker's dirty dozen from the author of *Wet Dreams.* Wild men build up steam until they finally let loose. No-nonsense guys bear down hard on each other as they work their way toward release in this finely detailed assortment of masculine fantasies.

Wet Dreams $4.95/142-X

These tales take a hot look at the obsessions that keep men up all night—from simple skin-on-skin to more unusual pleasures. Provocative and affecting, this is a nightful of dreams you won't forget in the morning.

D.V. SADERO

Revolt of the Naked $4.95/261-2

In a distant galaxy, there are two classes of humans: Freemen and Nakeds. Freemen are full citizens in this system, which allows for the buying and selling of Nakeds at whim. Nakeds live only to serve their Masters, and obey every sexual order with haste and devotion. Until the day of revolution—when an army of sex toys rises in anger....

In the Alley $4.95/144-6

Twenty cut-to-the-chase yarns inspired by the all-American male. Hardworking men—from cops to carpenters—bring their own special skills and impressive tools to the most satisfying job of all: capturing and breaking the male sexual beast. Hot, incisive and way over the top!

GARY BOWEN

Man Hungry $5.95/374-0

By the author of *Diary of a Vampire*. A riveting collection of stories from one of gay erotica's new stars. Dipping into a variety of genres, Bowen crafts tales of lust unlike anything being published today. Men of every type imaginable—and then some—work up a sweat for readers whose lusts know no bounds.

KYLE STONE

Hot Bauds $5.95/285-X

The author of *Fantasy Board* and *The Initiation of PB 500* combed cyberspace for the hottest fantasies of the world's horniest hackers. From bulletin boards called Studs, The Mine Shaft, Back Door and the like, Stone has assembled the first collection of the raunchy erotica so many gay men cruise the Information Superhighway for. Plug in—and get ready to download....

Fantasy Board $4.95/212-4

The author of the scalding sci-fi adventures of PB 500 explores the more foreseeable future—through the intertwined lives (and private parts) of a collection of randy computer hackers. On the Lambda Gate BBS, every hot and horny male is in search of a little virtual satisfaction.contented.

The Citadel $4.95/198-5

The thundering sequel to *The Initiation of PB 500*. Having proven himself worthy of his stunning master, Micah—now known only as '500'—will face new challenges and hardships after his entry into the forbidding Citadel. Only his master knows what awaits—and whether Micah will again distinguish himself as the perfect instrument of pleasure....

Rituals $4.95/168-3

Via a computer bulletin board, a young man finds himself drawn into a series of sexual rites that transform him into the willing slave of a mysterious stranger. Gradually, all vestiges of his former life are thrown off, and he learns to live for his Master's touch.... A high-tech fable of sexual surrender.

The Initiation PB 500 $4.95/141-1

He is a stranger on their planet, unschooled in their language, and ignorant of their customs. But this man, Micah—now known only by his number—will soon be trained in every last detail of erotic personal service. And, once nurtured and transformed into the perfect physical specimen, he must begin proving himself worthy of the master who has chosen him.... A scalding sci-fi epic, continued in *The Citadel*.

PHIL ANDROS

The Joy Spot $5.95/301-5

"Andros gives to the gay mind what Tom of Finland gives the gay eye—this is archetypal stuff. There's none better."

—John F. Karr, *Manifest Reader*

A classic from one of the founding fathers of gay porn. *The Joy Spot* looks at some of Andros' favorite types—cops, servicemen, truck drivers—and the sleaze they love. Nothing's too rough, and these men are always ready. So get ready to give it up—or have it taken by force!

ROBERT BAHR

Sex Show $4.95/225-6

Luscious dancing boys. Brazen, explicit acts. Unending stimulation. Take a seat, and get very comfortable, because the curtain's going up on a show no discriminating appetite can afford to miss. And the award for Best Performer...is up to you....

"BIG" BILL JACKSON

Eighth Wonder $4.95/200-0

"Big" Bill Jackson's always the randiest guy in town—no matter what town he's in. From the bright lights and back rooms of New York to the open fields and sweaty bods of a small Southern town, "Big" Bill always manages to cause a scene, and the more actors he can involve, the better! Like the man's name says, he's got more than enough for everyone, and turns nobody down....

JASON FURY

The Rope Above, the Bed Below $4.95/269-8

The irresistible Jason Fury returns—and if you thought his earlier adventures were hot, this volume will blow you away! Once again, our built, blond hero finds himself in the oddest—and most compromising—positions imaginable.

Eric's Body $4.95/151-9

Meet Jason Fury—blond, blue-eyed and up for anything. Perennial favorites in the gay press, Fury's sexiest tales are collected in book form for the first time. Ranging from the bittersweet to the surreal, these stories follow the irresistible Jason through sexual adventures unlike any you have ever read....

JOHN ROWBERRY

Lewd Conduct $4.95/3091-1

Flesh-and-blood men vie for power, pleasure and surrender in each of these feverish stories, and no one walks away from his steamy encounter unsated. Rowberry's men are unafraid to push the limits of civilized behavior in search of the elusive and empowering conquest.

LARS EIGHNER

Whispered in the Dark $5.95/286-8

Lars Eighner continues to produce gay fiction whose quality rivals the best in the genre. *Whispered in the Dark* continues to demonstrate Eighner's unique combination of strengths: poetic descriptive power, an unfailing ear for dialogue, and a finely tuned feeling for the nuances of male passion. *Whispered in the Dark* reasserts Eighner's claim to mastery of the gay erotica genre.

American Prelude $4.95/170-5

Another volume of irresistible Eighner tales. Praised by *The New York Times*, Eighner is widely recognized as one of our best, most exciting gay writers. What the *Times* won't admit, however, is that he is also one of gay erotica's true masters—and *American Prelude* shows why.

Bayou Boy $4.95/3084-9

Another collection of well-tuned stories from one of our finest writers. Witty and incisive, each tale explores the many ways men work up a sweat in the steamy Southwest. *Bayou Boy* also includes the "Houston Streets" stories—sexy, touching tales of growing up gay in a fast-changing world. Street smart and razor sharp—and guaranteed to warm the coldest night!

B.M.O.C. $4.95/3077-6

In a college town known as "the Athens of the Southwest," studs of every stripe are up all night—studying, naturally. In *B.M.O.C.*, Lars Eighner includes the very best of his short stories, sure to appeal to the collegian in every man. Relive university life the way it was *supposed* to be, with a cast of handsome honor students majoring in Human Homosexuality.

CALDWELL/EIGHNER

QSFx2   **$5.95/278-7**

One volume of the wickedest, wildest, other-worldliest yarns from two master storytellers—Clay Caldwell and Lars Eighner, the highly-acclaimed author of *Travels With Lizbeth*. Both eroticists take a trip to the furthest reaches of the sexual imagination, sending back ten stories proving that as much as things change, one thing will always remain the same....

AARON TRAVIS

In the Blood   **$5.95/283-3**

Written when Travis had just begun to explore the true power of the erotic imagination, these stories laid the groundwork for later masterpieces. Among the many rewarding rarities included in this volume: "In the Blood"—a heart-pounding descent into sexual vampirism, written with the furious erotic power that has distinguished Travis' work from the beginning.

The Flesh Fables   **$4.95/243-4**

One of Travis' best collections, finally rereleased. *The Flesh Fables* includes "Blue Light," his most famous story, as well as other masterpieces that established him as the erotic writer to watch. And watch carefully, because Travis always buries a surprise somewhere beneath his scorching detail....

Slaves of the Empire   **$4.95/3054-7**

The return of an undisputed classic from this master of the erotic genre. "*Slaves of the Empire* is a wonderful mythic tale. Set against the backdrop of the exotic and powerful Roman Empire, this wonderfully written novel explores the timeless questions of light and dark in male sexuality. Travis has shown himself expert in manipulating the most primal themes and images. The locale may be the ancient world, but these are the slaves and masters of our time...."   —John Preston

Big Shots   **$4.95/112-8**

Two fierce tales in one electrifying volume. In *Beirut,* Travis tells the story of ultimate military power and erotic subjugation; *Kip,* Travis' hypersexed and sinister take on *film noir,* appears in unexpurgated form for the first time—including the final, overwhelming chapter. Unforgettable acts and relentless passions dominate these chronicles of unimaginable lust—as seen from the points of view of raging, powerful men, and the bottomless submissives who yield to their desires. From a legendary talent comes one of our rawest, most unrelenting titles.

Exposed   **$4.95/126-8**

A volume of shorter Travis tales, each providing a unique glimpse of the horny gay male in his natural environment! Cops, college jocks, ancient Romans—even Sherlock Holmes and his loyal Watson—cruise these pages, fresh from the throbbing pen of one of our hottest authors.

Beast of Burden   **$4.95/105-5**

Five ferocious tales from a master of lascivious prose. Innocents surrender to the brutal sexual mastery of their superiors, as taboos are shattered and replaced with the unwritten rules of masculine conquest. Intense, extreme—and totally Travis.

CLAY CALDWELL

Ask Ol' Buddy   **$5.95/346-5**

One of the most popular novels of this legendary gay eroticist. Set in the underground SM world, Caldwell takes you on a journey of discovery—where men initiate one another into the secrets of the rawest sexual realm of all. And when each stud's initiation is complete, he takes his places among the masters—eager to take part in the training of another hungry soul...

Service, Stud $5.95/336-8

From the author of the sexy sci-fi epic *All-Stud*, comes another look at the
gay future. The setting is the Los Angeles of a distant future. Here the all-
male populace is divided between the served and the servants—an arrange-
ment guaranteeing the erotic satisfaction of all involved. Until one young stud
challenges authority, and the sexual rules it so rigidly enforces....

Stud Shorts $5.95/320-1

"If anything, Caldwell's charm is more powerful, his nostalgia more
poignant, the horniness he captures more sweetly, achingly acute than
ever."   —Aaron Travis

A new collection of this legendary writer's latest sex-fiction. With his custom-
ary candor, Caldwell tells all about cops, cadets, truckers, farmboys (and many
more) in these dirty jewels.

Tailpipe Trucker $5.95/296-5

With *Tailpipe Trucker*, Clay Caldwell set the cornerstone of "trucker
porn"—a story revolving around the age-old fantasy of horny men on the
road. In prose as free and unvarnished as a cross-country highway, Caldwell
tells the truth about Trag and Curly—two men hot for the feeling of sweaty
manflesh.

Queers Like Us $4.95/262-0

"This is Caldwell at his most charming."   —Aaron Travis

For years the name Clay Caldwell has been synonymous with the hottest,
most finely crafted gay tales available. *Queers Like Us* is one of his best: the
story of a randy mailman's trek through a landscape of willing, available studs.

All-Stud $4.95/104-7

An incredible, erotic trip into the gay future. This classic, sex-soaked tale
takes place under the watchful eye of Number Ten: an omniscient figure who
has decreed unabashed promiscuity as the law of his all-male land. Men exist
to serve men, and all surrender to state-sanctioned fleshly indulgence.

H O D D Y   A L L E N

Al $5.95/302-3

Al is a remarkable young man. With his long brown hair, bright green eyes
and eagerness to please, many would consider him the perfect submissive.
Many would like to mark him as their own—but it is at that point that Al
stops. One day Al relates the entire astounding tale of his life....

1 8 0 0 9 0 6 - H U N K

**Hardcore phone action for *real* men. A scorching assembly of
studs is waiting for your call—and eager to give you the head-
trip of your life! Totally live, guaranteed one-on-one encounters.
(Must be over 18.) No credit card needed. $3.98 per minute.**

K E Y   L I N C O L N

Submission Holds $4.95/266-3

A bright young talent unleashes his first collection of gay erotica. From tough
to tender, the men between these covers stop at nothing to get what they
want. These sweat-soaked tales show just how bad boys can really get....

T O M   B A C C H U S

Rahm $5.95/315-5

A volume spanning the many ages of hardcore queer lust—from Creation to
the modern day. The imagination of Tom Bacchus brings to life an extraordi-
nary assortment of characters, from the Father of Us All to the cowpoke next
door, the early gay literati to rude, queercore mosh rats. No one is better than
Bacchus at staking out sexual territory with a swagger and a sly grin.

Bone $4.95/177-2

Queer musings from the pen of one of today's hottest young talents. A fresh
outlook on fleshly indulgence yields more than a few pleasant surprises.
Horny Tom Bacchus maps out the tricking ground of a new generation.

VINCE GILMAN

The Slave Prince $4.95/199-3

A runaway royal learns the true meaning of power when he comes under the
hand of Korat—a man well-versed in the many ways of subjugating a young
man to his relentless sexual appetite.

BOB VICKERY

Skin Deep $4.95/265-5

Talk about "something for everyone!" *Skin Deep* contains so many varied
beauties no one will go away unsatisfied. No tantalizing morsel of manflesh is
overlooked—or left unexplored! Beauty may be only skin deep, but a handful
of beautiful skin is a tempting proposition.

EDITED BY DAVID LAURENTS

Wanderlust: Homoerotic Tales of Travel $5.95/395-3

A volume dedicated to the special pleasures of faraway places. Gay men have
always had a special interest in travel—and not only for the scenic vistas.
Including work by such renowned writers as Michael Lassell, Felice Picano,
Aaron Travis and Lars Eighner, *Wanderlust* celebrates the freedom of the
open road, and the allure of men who stray from the beaten path....

The Badboy Book of Erotic Poetry $5.95/382-1

Over fifty of gay literature's biggest talents are here represented by their
hottest verse. Both learned and stimulating, *The Badboy Book of Erotic
Poetry* restores eros to its rightful place of honor in contemporary gay writing.

JAMES MEDLEY

Huck and Billy $4.95/245-0

Young love is always the sweetest, always the most sorrowful. Young lust, on
the other hand, knows no bounds—and is often the hottest of one's life! Huck
and Billy explore the desires that course through their young male bodies,
determined to plumb the lusty depths of passion. Sweet and hot. Very hot.

LARRY TOWNSEND

Beware the God Who Smiles $5.95/321-X

A torrid time-travel tale from one of gay erotica's most notorious writers. Two
lusty young Americans are transported to ancient Egypt—where they are
embroiled in regional warfare and taken as slaves by marauding barbarians.
The key to escape from this brutal bondage lies in their own rampant libidos,
and urges as old as time itself.

The Construction Worker $5.95/298-1

A young, hung construction worker is sent to a building project in Central
America, where he is shocked to find some ancient and unusual traditions in
practice. In this isolated location, man-to-man sex is the accepted norm. The
young stud quickly fits right in (and quite snugly)—until he senses that
beneath the constant sexual shenanigans there moves an almost supernatural
force. Soon, nothing is what it seems....

2069 Trilogy (This one-volume collection only $6.95) 244-2

For the first time, Larry Townsend's early science-fiction trilogy appears in
one volume! Set in a future world, the *2069 Trilogy* includes the tight plotting
and shameless male sexual pleasure that established him as one of gay eroti-
ca's first masters. This special one-volume edition available only from Badboy.

Mind Master $4.95/209-4

Who better to explore the territory of erotic dominance and submission than an author who helped define the genre—and knows that ultimate mastery always transcends the physical.

The Long Leather Cord $4.95/201-9

Chuck's stepfather is an enigma: never lacking in money or clandestine male visitors with whom he enacts intense sexual rituals. As Chuck comes to terms with his own savage desires, he begins to unravel his stepfather's mystery.

Man Sword $4.95/188-8

The *tres gai* tale of France's King Henri III. Unimaginably spoiled by his mother—the infamous Catherine de Medici—Henri is groomed from a young age to assume the throne of France. Along the way, he encounters enough sexual schemers and randy politicos to alter one's picture of history forever!

The Faustus Contract $4.95/167-5

Two attractive young men desperately need $1000. Will do anything. Travel OK. Danger OK. Call anytime... Two cocky young hustlers get more than they bargained for in this story of lust and its discontents.

The Gay Adventures of Captain Goose $4.95/169-1

The hot and tender young Jerome Gander is sentenced to serve aboard the *H.M.S. Faerigold*—a ship manned by the most hardened, unrepentant criminals. In no time, Gander becomes well-versed in the ways of men at sea, and the *Faerigold* becomes the most notorious ship of its day.

Chains $4.95/158-6

Picking up street punks has always been risky, but in Larry Townsend's classic *Chains*, it sets off a string of events that must be read to be believed. One of Townsend's most remarkable works.

Kiss of Leather $4.95/161-6

A look at the acts and attitudes of an earlier generation of leathermen, *Kiss of Leather* is full to bursting with the gritty, raw action that has distinguished Townsend's work for years. Pain and pleasure mix in this tightly-plotted tale.

Run No More $4.95/152-7

The continuation of Larry Townsend's legendary *Run, Little Leather Boy*. This volume follows the further adventures of Townsend's leatherclad narrator as he travels every sexual byway available to the S/M male.

Run, Little Leather Boy $4.95/143-8

The classic story of one young man's sexual awakening. A chronic under-achiever, Wayne seems to be going nowhere fast. When his father puts him to work for a living, Wayne soon finds himself bored with the everyday—and increasingly drawn to the masculine intensity of a dark sexual underground....

The Scorpius Equation $4.95/119-5

Set in the far future, *The Scorpius Equation* is the story of a man caught between the demands of two galactic empires. Our randy hero must match wits—and more—with the incredible forces that rule his world.

The Sexual Adventures of Sherlock Holmes $4.95/3097-0

Holmes' most satisfying adventures, from the unexpurgated memoirs of the faithful Mr. Watson. "A Study in Scarlet" is transformed to expose Mrs. Hudson as a man in drag, the Diogenes Club as an S/M arena, and clues only Sherlock Holmes could piece together. A baffling tale of sex and mystery.

F L E D E R M A U S

Flederfiction: Stories of Men and Torture $5.95/355-4

Fifteen blistering paeans to men and their suffering. Fledermaus unleashes his most thrilling tales of punishment in this special volume designed with Badboy readers in mind. No less an authority than Larry Townsend introduces this volume of Fledermaus' best work.

DONALD VINING

Cabin Fever and Other Stories $5.95/338-4

Eighteen blistering stories in celebration of the most intimate of male bonding. From Native Americans to Buckingham Palace sentries, suburban husbands to kickass bikers—time after time, Donald Vining's men succumb to nature, and reaffirm both love and lust in modern gay life.

Praise for Donald Vining:

"Realistic but upbeat, blunt but graceful, serious but witty... demonstrates the wisdom experience combined with insight and optimism can create."
—*Bay Area Reporter*

DEREK ADAMS

My Double Life $5.95/314-7

Every man leads a double life, dividing his hours between the mundanities of the day and the outrageous pursuits of the night. In this, his second collection of stories, the author of *Boy Toy* and creator of sexy P.I. Miles Diamond shines a little light on what men do when no one's looking.

Boy Toy $4.95/260-4

Poor Brendan Callan—sent to the Brentwood Academy against his will, he soon finds himself the guinea pig of a crazed geneticist. Brendan becomes irresistibly alluring—a talent designed for endless pleasure, but coveted by others for the most unsavory means....

Heat Wave $4.95/159-4

"His body was draped in baggy clothes, but there was hardly any doubt that they covered anything less than perfection.... His slacks were cinched tight around a narrow waist, and the rise of flesh pushing against the thin fabric promised a firm, melon-shaped ass...."

Miles Diamond and the Demon of Death $4.95/251-5

Derek Adams' gay gumshoe returns for further adventures. Miles always find himself in the stickiest situations—with any stud whose path he crosses! His adventures with "The Demon of Death" promise another carnal carnival.

The Adventures of Miles Diamond $4.95/118-7

"The Case of the Missing Twin" promises to be a most rewarding case, packed as it is with randy studs. Miles sets about uncovering all as he tracks down the elusive and delectable Daniel Travis....

KELVIN BELIELE

If the Shoe Fits $4.95/223-X

An essential and winning volume of tales exploring a world where randy boys can't help but do what comes naturally—as often as possible! Sweaty male bodies grapple in pleasure, proving the old adage: if the shoe fits, one might as well slip right in....

VICTOR TERRY

WHiPs $4.95/254-X

Connoisseurs of gay writing have known Victor Terry's work for some time. Cruising for a hot man? You'd better be, because one way or another, these WHiPs—officers of the Wyoming Highway Patrol—are gonna pull you over for a little impromptu interrogation....

MAX EXANDER

Deeds of the Night: Tales of Eros and Passion $5.95/348-1

MAXimum porn! Exander's a writer who's seen it all—and is more than happy to describe every inch of it in pulsating detail. From the man behind *Mansex* and *Leathersex*—two whirlwind tours of the hypermasculine libido—comes another unrestrained volume of sweat-soaked fantasies.

Leathersex $4.95/210-8

Another volume of hard-hitting tales from merciless Max Exander. This time he focuses on the leatherclad lust that draws together only the most willing and talented of tops and bottoms—for an all-out orgy of limitless surrender and control....

Mansex $4.95/160-8

"Tex was all his name implied: tall, lanky but muscular, with reddish-blond hair and a handsome, chiseled face that was somewhat leathered. Mark was the classic leatherman: a huge, dark stud in chaps, with a big black moustache, hairy chest and enormous muscles. Exactly the kind of men Todd liked—strong, hunky, masculine, ready to take control...." Rough sex for rugged men.

TOM CAFFREY

Hitting Home $4.95/222-1

One of our newest Badboys weighs in with a scorching collection of stories. Titillating and compelling, the stories in *Hitting Home* make a strong case for there being only one thing on a man's mind.

TORSTEN BARRING

Prisoners of Torquemada $5.95/252-3

The infamously unsparing Torsten Barring (*The Switch, Peter Thornwell, Shadowman*) weighs in with another volume sure to push you over the edge. How cruel is the "therapy" practiced at Casa Torquemada? Rest assured that Barring is just the writer to evoke such steamy malevolence.

Shadowman $4.95/178-0

From spoiled Southern aristocrats to randy youths sowing wild oats at the local picture show, Barring's imagination works overtime in these vignettes of homolust—past, present and future.

Peter Thornwell $4.95/149-7

Follow the exploits of Peter Thornwell as he goes from misspent youth to scandalous stardom, all thanks to an insatiable libido and love for the lash. Peter and his sex-crazed sidekicks find themselves pursued by merciless men from all walks of life in this torrid take on Horatio Alger.

The Switch $4.95/3061-X

Sometimes a man needs a good whipping, and *The Switch* certainly makes a case! Laced with images of men "in too-tight Levi's, with the faces of angels... and the bodies of devils." Packed with hot studs and unrelenting passions.

BERT McKENZIE

Fringe Benefits $5.95/354-6

From the pen of a widely published short story writer comes a volume of highly immodest tales. Not afraid of getting down and dirty, McKenzie produces some of today's most visceral sextales. Learn the real benefits of working long and hard....

SONNY FORD

Reunion in Florence $4.95/3070-9

Captured by Turks, Adrian and Tristan will do anything to save their heads. When Tristan is threatened by a Sultan's jealousy, Adrian begins his quest for the only man alive who can replace Tristan as the object of the Sultan's lust. The two soon learn to rely on their wild sexual imaginations.

ROGER HARMAN

First Person $4.95/179-9

A highly personal collection. Each story here takes the form of an uncensored confessional—told by men who've got plenty to confess! From the "first time ever" to firsts of different kinds, *First Person* tells truths too hot to be purely fiction.

CHRISTOPHER MORGAN

Muscle Bound $4.95/3028-8

In the New York City bodybuilding scene, country boy Tommy joins forces with sexy Will Rodriguez in a battle of wits and biceps at the hottest gym in Greenwich Village, where the weak are bound and crushed by iron-pumping gods.

SEAN MARTIN

Scrapbook $4.95/224-8

Imagine a book filled with only the best, most vivid remembrances...a book brimming with every hot, sexy encounter its pages can hold... Now you need only open up *Scrapbook* to know that such a volume really exists....

CARO SOLES & STAN TAL

Bizarre Dreams $4.95/187-X

An anthology of stirring voices dedicated to exploring the dark side of human fantasy. Including such BADBOY favorites as John Preston, Lars Eighner, and Kyle Stone, *Bizarre Dreams* brings together the most talented practitioners of "dark fantasy": the most forbidden sexual realm of all.

J. A. GUERRA

Badboy Fantasies $4.95/3049-0

When love eludes them—lust will do! Thrill-seeking men caught up in vivid dreams and dark mysteries—these are the brief encounters you'll pant and gasp over in *Badboy Fantasies*.

Slow Burn $4.95/3042-3

Welcome to the Body Shoppe, where men's lives cross in the pursuit of muscle. Torsos get lean and hard, pecs widen, and stomachs ripple in these sexy stories of the power and perils of physical perfection.

Men at Work $4.95/3027-X

He's the most gorgeous man you have ever seen. You yearn for his touch at night in your empty bed; but he's your co-worker! A collection of eight sizzling stories of man-to-man on-the-job training.

DAVE KINNICK

Sorry I Asked $4.95/3090-3

Unexpurgated interviews with gay porn's rank and file. Dave Kinnick, long-time video reviewer for *Advocate Men*, gets personal with the men behind (and under) the "stars," and reveals the dirt and details of the porn business.

MICHAEL LOWENTHAL, ED.

The BADBOY Erotic Library Volume I $4.95/190-X

A Secret Life, Imre, Sins of the Cities of the Plain, Teleny and *more*—the hottest sections of these perennial favorites come together for the first time.

The BADBOY Erotic Library Volume II $4.95/211-6

This time, selections are taken from *Mike and Me* and *Muscle Bound*, *Men at Work*, *Badboy Fantasies*, and *Slowburn*.

ERIC BOYD

Mike and Me $5.95/419-4

Mike joined the gym squad to bulk up on muscle. Little did he know he'd be turning on every sexy muscle jock in Minnesota! Hard bodies collide in a series of workouts designed to generate a whole lot more than rips and cuts.

Mike and the Marines $5.95/347-3

Mike and Me was one of Badboy's earliest hits, and now readers can revel in another sexy extravaganza. This time, Mike takes on America's most elite corp. of studs—running into more than a few good men!

ANONYMOUS

A Secret Life $4.95/3017-2
Meet Master Charles: only eighteen, and *quite* innocent, until his arrival at the Sir Percival's Royal Academy, where the daily lessons are supplemented with a crash course in pure, sweet sexual heat!

Sins of the Cities of the Plain $5.95/322-8
Indulge yourself in the scorching memoirs of young man-about-town Jack Saul. From his earliest erotic moments with Jerry in the dark of his bedchamber, to his shocking dalliances with the lords and "ladies" of British high society, Jack's positively *sinful* escapades grow wilder with every chapter!

Imre $4.95/3019-9
What dark secrets, what fiery passions lay hidden behind strikingly beautiful Lieutenant Imre's emerald eyes? An extraordinary lost classic of fantasy, obsession, gay erotic desire, and romance in a tiny town on the eve of WWI.

Teleny $4.95/3020-2
A dark Victorian classic, often attributed to Oscar Wilde. A young stud of independent means seeks only a succession of voluptuous and forbidden pleasures, but instead finds love and tragedy when he becomes embroiled in a mysterious cult devoted to fulfilling only the very darkest of fantasies.

PAT CALIFIA

The Sexpert $4.95/3034-2
The sophisticated gay man knows that he can turn to one authority for answers to virtually any question on the subjects of intimacy and sexual performance. Straight from the pages of *Advocate Men* comes The Sexpert, responding to real-life sexual concerns with uncanny wisdom and a razor wit.

HARD CANDY

RED JORDAN AROBATEAU

Dirty Pictures $6.95/345-7
"The grafitti artist of lesbian literature."
—Lee Lynch
Another red-hot tale from lesbian sensation Red Jordan Arobateau. *Dirty Pictures* tells the story of a lonely butch tending bar—and the femme she finally calls her own. With the same precision that made *Lucy and Mickey* a breakout debut, Arobateau tells a love story that's the flip-side of "lesbian chic." Not to be missed.

Lucy and Mickey $6.95/311-2
"Both deeply philosophical and powerfully erotic. Star-crossed and horny as hell, Mickey and Lucy endure a life that few lesbian novelists have the know-how—or the balls—to depict... Most of all this novel is about Mickey, a pugnacious butch who trades her powerlessness on the streets for prowess between the sheets. *Lucy and Mickey* is...a necessary reminder to all who blissfully—some may say ignorantly—ride the wave of lesbian chic into the mainstream."
—Heather Findlay, editor-in-chief of *Girlfriend*

LARS EIGHNER

Gay Cosmos $6.95/236-
A thought-provoking volume from widely acclaimed author Lars Eighner. Eighner has distinguished himself as not only one of America's most accomplished new voices, but a solid-seller—his erotic titles alone have become bestsellers and classics of the genre. *Gay Cosmos* argues passionately for acceptance of homosexuality by society.

JAMES COLTON

Todd $6.95/312-0

A classic returns. With *Todd*, Colton took on the complexities of American race relations, becoming one of the first writers to explore interracial love between two men. Set in 1971, Colton's novel examines the relationship of Todd and Felix, and the ways in which it is threatened by not only the era's politics, but the timeless stumbling block called The Former Lover. Tender and uncompromising, *Todd* takes on issues the gay community struggles with to this day.

The Outward Side $6.95/304-X

The return of a classic tale of one man's struggle with his deepest needs. Marc Lingard, a handsome, respected young minister, finds himself at a crossroads. The homophobic persecution of a local resident unearths Marc's long-repressed memories of a youthful love affair, and he is irrepressibly drawn to his forbidden urges.

STAN LEVENTHAL

Skydiving on Christopher Street $6.95/287-6

"Generosity, evenness, fairness to the reader, sensitivity—these are qualities that most contemporary writers take for granted or overrule with stylistics. In Leventhal's writing they not only stand out, they're positively addictive."   —Dennis Cooper

Aside from a hateful job, a hateful apartment, a hateful world and an increasingly hateful lover, life seems, well, all right for the protagonist of Stan Leventhal's latest novel. Having already lost most of his friends to AIDS, how could things get any worse? But things soon do, and he's forced to endure much more before finding a new strength. A touching, eloquent tribute to the human spirit.

FELICE PICANO

Men Who Loved Me $6.95/274-4

In 1966, at the tender-but-bored age of twenty-two, Felice Picano abandoned New York, determined to find true love in Europe. Almost immediately, he encounters Djanko—an exquisite prodigal who sweeps Felice off his feet with the endless string of extravagant parties, glamorous clubs and glittering premieres that made up Rome's *dolce vita*. When the older (slightly) and wiser (vastly) Picano returns to New York at last, he plunges into the city's thriving gay community—experiencing the frenzy and heartbreak that came to define Greenwich Village society in the 1970s. Lush and warm, *Men Who Loved Me* is a matchless portrait of an unforgettable decade.

"Zesty... spiked with adventure and romance.... a distinguished and humorous portrait of a vanished age."   —*Publishers Weekly*

"A stunner... captures the free-wheeling spirit of an era."
                                                        —*The Advocate*

"Rich, engaging, engrossing... a ravishingly exotic romance."
                                                        —*New York Native*

ORDERING IS EASY!

MC/VISA orders can be placed by calling our toll-free number

PHONE 800 375-2356/FAX 212 986-7355

or mail the coupon below to:

MASQUERADE BOOKS

DEPT. X74A, 801 SECOND AVENUE, NY, NY 10017

BUY ANY FOUR BOOKS AND CHOOSE ONE ADDITIONAL BOOK, OF EQUAL OR LESSER VALUE, AS YOUR FREE GIFT.

QTY.	TITLE	NO.	PRICE
			FREE
			FREE

X74A		SUBTOTAL	
	POSTAGE and HANDLING		

We Never Sell, Give or Trade Any Customer's Name.   **TOTAL**

In the U.S., please add $1.50 for the first book and 75¢ for each additional book; in Canada, add $2.00 for the first book and $1.25 for each additional book. Foreign countries: add $4.00 for the first book and $2.00 for each additional book. No C.O.D. orders. Please make all checks payable to Masquerade Books. Payable in U.S. currency only. New York state residents add 8¼% sales tax. Please allow 4-6 weeks delivery.

NAME _____

ADDRESS _____

CITY _____ STATE _____ ZIP _____

TEL ( ) _____

PAYMENT: ☐ CHECK ☐ MONEY ORDER ☐ VISA ☐ MC

CARD NO. _____ EXP. DATE _____